CONQUER YOUR BAD HABITS

DANIEL G. AMEN, MD
#1 *NEW YORK TIMES* BESTSELLING AUTHOR

CONQUER YOUR BAD HABITS

SECRETS TO LONG-LASTING CHANGE

TYNDALE
REFRESH®

Think Well. Live Well. Be Well.

Visit Tyndale online at tyndale.com.

Visit Daniel G. Amen, MD, at danielamenmd.com.

Tyndale, Tyndale's quill logo, *Tyndale Refresh*, and the Tyndale Refresh logo are registered trademarks of Tyndale House Ministries. Tyndale Refresh is a nonfiction imprint of Tyndale House Publishers, Carol Stream, Illinois.

Conquer Your Bad Habits: Secrets to Long-Lasting Change

Cover design by Libby Dykstra

Adapted primarily from *Your Brain Is Always Listening*, published in 2021 under ISBN 978-1-4964-3820-1. Additional content adapted from *30% Happier in 30 Days*, published in 2023 under ISBN 978-1-4964-7234-2; *Change Your Brain Every Day*, published in 2023 under ISBN 978-1-4964-5457-7; *The End of Mental Illness*, published in 2020 under ISBN 978-1-4964-3815-7; *Feel Better Fast and Make It Last*, published in 2018 under ISBN 978-1-4962-2565-2; and *You, Happier*, published in 2022 under ISBN 978-1-4964-5452-2.

Published in association with the literary agency of WordServe Literary Group, www.wordserveliterary.com.

For information about special discounts for bulk purchases, please contact Tyndale House Publishers at csresponse@tyndale.com, or call 1-855-277-9400.

ISBN 979-8-4005-1177-6

Printed in the United States of America

32 31 30 29 28 27 26
7 6 5 4 3 2 1

MEDICAL DISCLAIMER

Contents

INTRODUCTION

AS EASY AS CHANGING A LIGHT BULB

Until you make the unconscious conscious,
it will direct your life and you will call it fate.

ATTRIBUTED TO CARL JUNG

HABITS PRETTY MUCH RUN OUR LIVES. Whether it's telling our children we love them at the end of phone calls; making our spouse an unsweetened, almond milk decaf cappuccino in the morning (I do this for my wife every morning to show her I love her); brushing our teeth; flossing; shaving; blow-drying our hair (well . . . not me); showering; feeding our pets; putting away the dishes; closing cabinet doors; taking out the trash; or doing the laundry a certain way, habits are behaviors that have become so automated, we barely need to think about them.

Some habits—like exercising regularly, eating healthy, and carving out time to spend with loved ones—move our lives forward in good ways, while others—like overindulging, procrastinating, interrupting, and incessant nitpicking—can lead to trouble with our health, our relationships, and our careers.

Odds are, you've tried to change your bad habits before and failed (possibly more than once), leading you to believe that you *can't* change—at this point you simply are who you are and that's that. In fact, there's a classic joke in psychiatric circles. Maybe you've heard it. It goes, "How many psychiatrists does it take to change a light bulb? The answer: One, but the light bulb really has to *want* to change."

The good news is . . . it *is* possible to change your behavior and conquer your bad habits once and for all—and the secret lies within the three pounds of tissue nestled between your ears—that's right, your brain.

Let me explain.

Most people think of habits as a single task, but they are generally made up of many smaller behaviors through a process called long-term potentiation. Long-term potentiation occurs when the brain learns something new, causing networks of brain cells to make new connections.

Early in the learning process (say, the first time you reach for a sugary snack during a stressful moment or drum your fingers on the table when bored), the connections are weak, but over time, as those behaviors are repeated, the networks in your brain become stronger, until eventually, they become automatic, reflexive, or—you guessed it—*habitual.*

However, because your brain does what you train it to do, just as you trained your brain to normalize bad behaviors, you can also train it to turn those bad habits into good ones by creating new, healthier connections. And over the course of the next several chapters, I'm going to show you how to do just that!

Helping people change their bad behaviors has been my passion as a psychiatrist for the past four decades. And since 1991, my team at Amen Clinics and I have built the world's largest database of single photon emission computed tomography or SPECT (which is basically a fancy way of saying we create 3D images that highlight blood flow and activity within the brain), totaling more than 250,000 scans on patients from 155 countries. We have seen patients as young as nine months and as old as 105 years, and our SPECT brain imaging work has taught us many important lessons about the daily practices and habits that lead to healthy brains and healthy lifestyles.

And now I'm going to pass some of that learning on to you, so you can retrain your brain and eliminate your negative behaviors once and for all, and live a happier, healthier life.

Ready? Good.

Let's get started.

Daniel G. Amen, MD

CHAPTER 1

YOUR BRAIN—A VERY BRIEF PRIMER

BEFORE WE EMBARK on this life-changing journey together, it's important to briefly get acquainted with the six brain systems involved in running your life. Obviously, your brain is complicated and involves many different structures, but these six areas are particularly important as they work in concert to determine your behavior.

Cerebellum: Located at the back, bottom portion of the brain, it is only 10 percent of the brain's volume, yet it contains half of the brain's neurons or cells. It is involved in coordination, processing speed, cognitive processing, and language.

Inside View of the Brain

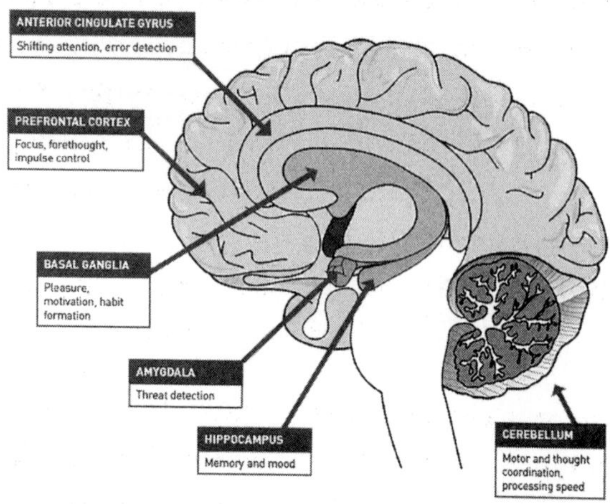

Hippocampus: About the size of your thumbs, your two hippocampi are found deep in the brain on the inside of your left and right temporal lobes. They are part of your emotional brain and help you feel happy or sad and are central to memory. They retain new information and store it for up to several weeks; if it is reinforced, you keep it longer.

Amygdala: This almond-shaped structure is found underneath the temples and behind the eyes; there is one on each side of the brain. Our amygdala is involved in emotion, threat detection, and aggression. When we get our feelings hurt, when we feel invisible, inadequate, angry, or ashamed, our amygdala activates, and we feel anxious, irritated, and out of sorts. Our amygdala is constantly scanning the world to protect us from danger, but our amygdala doesn't know the difference between danger in the present and danger in the past, a child in danger and a critical comment made by a coworker.

Anterior cingulate gyrus (ACG): Found deep within the frontal lobes, the anterior cingulate gyrus allows us to shift our attention, go from thought to thought, move from idea to idea, see options, go with the flow, and cooperate, which involves getting outside ourselves to help others. The ACG is also involved in error detection. If you come home and see the front door wide open, for example, even though you know you locked it, it triggers an appropriate danger reaction in your mind.

So how do you know when your anterior cingulate gyrus is in overdrive? Just for fun, put a checkmark next to the questions in the following list that apply to you.

- ☐ Do you dislike change?
- ☐ Do you tend to get stuck in loops of thinking?
- ☐ Do you struggle with repetitive, negative thoughts?
- ☐ Do you have difficulty seeing options in stressful situations?
- ☐ Do you tend to hold on to your own opinions and not listen to others?
- ☐ Do you get locked into a course of action, even though it may not be good for you?
- ☐ Do you tend to automatically say no without thinking?
- ☐ Do you get upset if you are surprised or if things don't go the way you expect they should?
- ☐ Do you struggle with compulsive behaviors, such as handwashing, checking locks, counting, or spelling?
- ☐ Do you tend to be oppositional or argumentative?

The more questions you checked, the more likely you have an ACG that is working too hard!

Basal ganglia (BG): Deep in the brain, the basal ganglia are involved with integrating thoughts, emotions, and movement, which is why we jump when we get excited or freeze when we become scared. The BG also help to shift and smooth motor behavior and are involved in habit formation.

Our research and that of others suggests that when the BG are overactive, people struggle with generalized anxiety, dislike uncertainty, and avoid conflict.[1] When the BG are underactive, people tend to have low motivation, poor handwriting, and trouble feeling pleasure.

Prefrontal cortex (PFC): Found in the front third of the brain, the prefrontal cortex plays a major role in executive functions, such as focus, forethought, judgment, planning, decision-making, and impulse control.

The PFC is larger in humans than any other animal, and it is the last part of the brain to develop. It is generally not finished maturing until people are in their mid- to late twenties. Knowing this, it is easier to understand why kids, teens, and young adults have lower executive function.

The prefrontal cortex acts as the brain's conscience, helping you match your behavior over time to reach your goals in a manner consistent with your morals and beliefs. It also sends signals to other parts of the brain to calm them down. When the PFC is healthy, it is like a conductor in an orchestra that gets the musicians to play together to create beautiful music.

Unless you are asleep, your prefrontal cortex is always watching over you, protecting you from your impulses and the first thoughts that come into your head. Sleep causes the prefrontal cortex to go offline, which is why your dreams are often unconstrained and wild.

Low activity causes the PFC to take a break and go on vacation, leaving you easily distracted, with low impulse control and empathy, or poor judgment. When your prefrontal cortex is hyperactive (the scientific term is *hyperfrontality*), you are always on guard, worrying, obsessively thinking, micromanaging, and being upset when things don't go your way. Hyperfrontality has been associated with obsessive-compulsive disorder, obsessive-compulsive personality trait (being rigid and inflexible, and having excessive self-control), and some forms of depression[2]—all psychological and social issues that make your relationships more difficult.

Take Care of Your Prefrontal Cortex So It Can Take Care of You

There is a constant dance between your prefrontal cortex (the boss that keeps everyone else on task), your amygdala (the part of your emotional brain that responds to threats), and your basal ganglia (where habits are shaped and stored). When your prefrontal cortex is weak, your impulses can take over, causing bad habits to form. That's why you must protect the part of the brain that protects you and pay attention to the following problems:

1. **Anything that lowers blood flow to the brain.** Blood is essential to life. It brings nourishment to every cell in your body and takes away waste. Research suggests that brain cells don't age; rather, it's your blood vessels that age![3] Anything that damages blood vessels damages

your brain and starves it of the nutrients it needs. Low blood flow is the number one predictor of Alzheimer's disease and is associated with ADD/ADHD, depression, and schizophrenia, a serious psychotic disorder. Things that decrease blood flow—such as high blood pressure, any form of vascular or heart disease, lack of exercise, and substances such as caffeine and nicotine—lower the function of the prefrontal cortex.

2. **Aging.** The older you get, the lower blood flow is to the prefrontal cortex. Brain imaging clearly shows that your brain typically becomes less active with age. This is why the older you get, the more serious you need to be about taking care of your brain.

3. **Inflammation**, which comes from the Latin word meaning to set a fire, is like having a low-level fire destroying your organs. Having low levels of the omega-3 fatty acids EPA and DHA in your bloodstream is associated with inflammation and linked to ADD/ADHD, a sign of prefrontal cortex dysfunction.

4. **Head trauma.** This is the most common cause of prefrontal cortex problems. In one study my team published, 94 percent of head injuries affected the frontal lobes.[4] The brain is soft, about the consistency of soft butter, and your skull is really hard with multiple sharp bony ridges. So protect your brain from injury by avoiding any activities that could cause you to hit your head. (Note: Do not let your children play tackle football or hit soccer balls with their heads.)

5. **Toxins**, including mold, heavy metals like lead, or other environmental toxins can damage the prefrontal cortex. Drugs and alcohol lower blood flow and function to the prefrontal cortex, which is why people tend to make poorer decisions when they are high, stoned, or drunk.

6. **Obesity** has been shown to lower prefrontal cortex function because it causes inflammation in your body; protect your weight.

7. **High or low blood sugar** can hurt the prefrontal cortex. High blood sugar (prediabetes

and diabetes) damages blood vessels and lowers function of the prefrontal cortex. Low blood sugar, from fasting or hypoglycemia, also lowers blood flow to the brain. The quality of your diet is critical to the health of your prefrontal cortex.

8. **Poor sleep**, including insomnia, sleep apnea, and sleeping pills can take the prefrontal cortex offline. An estimated 50 to 70 million Americans have sleep-related issues, according to the National Institutes of Health.[5] When you sleep, your brain cleans or washes itself. If sleep is disrupted, trash builds up in your brain, which damages your memory. Getting less than seven hours of sleep at night decreases the strength of your prefrontal cortex and is associated with weight issues, hypertension, and accidents. It may also cause trouble in your marriage because you are more likely to say something you wish you hadn't.

When your prefrontal cortex is healthy and strong, it can—like a good boss or supervisor—help direct and supervise the addition of healthy habits.

CHAPTER 2

ON YOUR MARK, LET'S SET . . . GOALS!

OVER THREE DECADES of studying the brain and working with patients who are trying to make major life changes, I have found that when you tell your brain what you want, your brain will help you make it happen.

You see, once the brain learns how to do something, it becomes wired to do it automatically and reflexively through a process called neuroplasticity. If, for example, you deal with pressure by drinking alcohol or lashing out at those around you, you are likely to continue that behavior whenever you feel stressed—unless you develop a new model of doing things to *rewire* your brain.

Of course, new learning and change take strategy, effort, and resources, which is why we often get stuck. I find this to be true in my own life and bet you do too. Depending on what you've taught your brain to do, neuroplasticity can help you develop and maintain good habits, or it can cause you to get stuck in ruts that steal portions of your life. If you were an anxious child, for example, anxiety built specific connecting highways (neural networks) in your brain, and unless you did something to rewire them, odds are, you still feel anxious as an adult.

That's why—in addition to using the BRIGHT MINDS strategies in appendix 1—you need to be intentional about telling your brain what you want it to do. Over the years, I have found that the patients who have the most success rewiring their brains are those who have clearly set goals.

With the brain, what you practice and reinforce becomes your reality. If you focus on negativity, you will feel depressed. If you focus on fear, you are likely to feel anxious. If you focus on achieving your goals, you are much more likely to reach them.

To help you establish these goals, I have developed a powerful yet simple motivation exercise that will help guide your thoughts, words, and actions. It is called the One Page Miracle,[1] and I call it that because I have seen this exercise quickly focus and change many people's lives.

The One Page Miracle will help guide your thoughts, words, and behaviors. Your One Page Miracle can help you quickly determine if they are helping you reach your goals or if they are hindering you from accomplishing what you want in life. It will also help you stay focused on your goals.

Here's how it works. On a piece of paper (or using the form that follows), clearly write (or, if you prefer to use your phone or computer, type) out your goals in each of the following areas: Relationships (spouse, parents, children, friends, neighbors), School/Work, Finances, and Self (physical, emotional, and spiritual health).

In each section, succinctly write out what's important to you in that area; write what you want, not what you don't want. Be positive, use the first person, and, if possible, include what you are currently doing to achieve these goals. For example:

What Do I Want? What Am I Doing to Make It Happen?

RELATIONSHIPS:

Spouse/Love: I want to be more present with my spouse, so I am making a point of turning off the TV and putting my phone away whenever we are talking or spending quality time together so I can focus solely on her.

Parents: I want my parents to be a bigger part of my kids' lives, so I am inviting them over once a week for dinner and a family game night.

Children: I want to be more supportive of my kids, so I am setting aside half an hour every night before they go to bed to ask them specific questions about their day, school, friends, etc.

Family/Friends: I want to eliminate toxic friends from my life and surround myself with positive people who love and support me. I'm trying to establish boundaries to limit my exposure to negative people and actively seek out encouragers.

Neighbors: I want to get to know my neighbors better, so I am going to start saying hello whenever I see them outside, learning their kids' and pets' names. I am thinking about hosting a get-to-know-you barbecue.

WORK: I would like to get promoted within my department, so I am going to ask my supervisor to help me identify any areas of improvement I might make.

SCHOOL: I want to finish my degree, so I am looking into night classes at the local community college.

FINANCES: I want to retire at 65, so I am going to meet with a financial advisor to help me pay down my existing debt and establish a budget that will allow me to contribute more to my 401(k).

SELF:

Physical Health: I want to lose weight, so I have enrolled in a healthy subscription meal plan program, have started walking two miles every morning, and have purchased a pair of jeans in my goal size to keep me motivated and on track!

Emotional Health: I want to limit the amount of negative news and information I see and hear every day, so I am going to take a 30-day social media fast.

Spiritual Health: I want to spend more time reading and studying God's Word, so I downloaded a reading plan to help me read through the entire Bible in a year and have joined a small group at church.

Now you try! Remember—keep it positive! And if you haven't started taking steps towards achieving these goals yet, just jot down a couple things you *can* start doing! If possible, try to choose action steps that are concrete and repeatable. The more we do something (like committing to walking two miles every day or reading the Bible every day), the faster our brain will learn the new behavior, and soon it will become habitual.

What Do I Want? What Am I Doing to Make It Happen?

RELATIONSHIPS:

Spouse/Love: ______________________

____

____

____

Parents: ______________________

____

____

____

Children: ______________________

____

____

____

Family/Friends: ______________________

____

____

____

Neighbors: ______________________

____

____

____

WORK:

SCHOOL:

FINANCES:

SELF:

Physical Health:

Emotional Health:

Spiritual Health:

Remember, your brain makes happen what it sees, so once you've got your One Page Miracle filled out, keep it someplace where you can see it every day, like your nightstand or on the refrigerator. You might even want to create a living document on your laptop, phone, or tablet that you can update as old goals are achieved and new goals come to mind!

Bottom line, when you give your prefrontal cortex some direction, your actions become more intentional, and it becomes much easier for you to change your behavior to get what you want.

So, make a habit of looking at your One Page Miracle every day, and start rewiring your brain to replace those bad habits and behaviors with good ones!

CHAPTER 3

5 SIMPLE STEPS TO CONQUERING YOUR BAD HABITS

EVERYONE HAS BAD HABITS. Whether it be smoking, biting your nails, overeating, telling little white lies, scrolling on your phone while driving, overspending, leaving projects until the last minute, not cleaning up after yourself at home, talking over other people, quitting as soon as a task becomes difficult, nitpicking, or oversleeping—we all have unhealthy or irritating behaviors that we have been engaging in for so long, they have become automatic.

But thanks to neuroplasticity, it is possible to retrain our brains to convert bad habits into good/healthy ones, and in just five simple steps!

In his book *Atomic Habits*, James Clear says that to create a new habit, make it obvious; know the cues; make the new habit attractive by giving rewards; make it easy to get into a new routine, the simpler the better; and make it satisfying.[1]

That's exactly what we're going to do!

As Simple as 1, 2, 3 (4 & 5)

Step 1: Identify the bad habit and start tracking it. Establishing a baseline of the unwanted habit and how often it occurs will help you track your progress.

For example, whenever I go to a restaurant, the waiter sets a basket of bread on the table. Seems harmless enough, right? But there's a reason they do that. Bread quickly turns to sugar in the stomach, causing an immediate spike in blood sugar and the hormone insulin, which, in turn, drives tryptophan into your brain, lowering blood flow to the prefrontal cortex, making you more likely to order additional food (especially high-calorie desserts) and overeat.

So in this case, the bad habit would be overeating, and it tends to come up whenever I am dining out at a restaurant.

Step 2: Identify the cues or triggers for the habit. When you notice an urge to do something (e.g., digging into the free bread at a restaurant), ask yourself questions such as these:

- What is the time of day?
- Where are you?
- Who are you with?
- How are you feeling?
- What is happening?

Answering these five questions will help you identify the cues or triggers to the behavior.

In my situation, the time of day would likely be evening, and I'd likely be with my spouse or a group of friends. The mood would be relaxed and happy, and the trigger would be—you guessed it—the waiter stopping by the table with a basket of freshly-baked bread.

Step 3: Identify the rewards or benefits of the behavior. Know what you are seeking. Is it pleasure, energy, excitement, happiness, relief, relaxation, acceptance, love, or something else? (Hint: Oftentimes the rewards you receive for bad behaviors are more immediate.)

In my case, the benefits of eating the freshly baked bread would be the pleasure I get from eating it, and the relaxation that comes from the tryptophan boost.

Step 4: Identify other ways to get the same or better benefits. How else could you get what you are looking for? Experiment with different options. Whenever you experience a bad habit trigger, substitute something else to see if you can get the same benefit but in a way that will serve your health and happiness rather than hurt it. In other words, love only behaviors that love you back. (Hint: The rewards you receive for replacing a bad habit with a good one are often long term.)

For example, whenever I catch myself wanting to nibble on something at a restaurant, I just ask for some carrot or celery sticks. They usually have them on hand for little kids. I just refuse the customary offer of ranch dressing to dip them in. It's still a treat, but instead of feeling bloated and tired, my body and brain get something that's good for them, and I get to experience a satisfying crunch!

Step 5: Build a new routine. Now that you know the cues and rewards, build a new routine(s) to get what you want (per your One Page Miracle goals). Focus on the rewards you will get without that bad habit, and keep it simple. For example:

- What is the habit you want to change? I want to stop overeating.
- What are the cues to the habit? It's evening, I'm at a restaurant with my spouse and friends, it's a relaxed atmosphere, and the waiter brings bread to the table.
- What rewards are you seeking? Immediate: fullness. Long-term: having a healthier lifestyle and better control over *my* eating habits.
- What new routine(s) can you build? I can ask the waiter to take the bread away to eliminate the temptation, and if I am still wanting a predinner snack, I can ask for a nice selection of healthy vegetables to munch on.

That's all there is to it! But be patient. Remember, it takes repetition for your brain to rewire itself and make new connections. Early in the learning process, these connections are going to be weak (I had to *really* think about saying no to the bread), but over time, as you continue to recognize the cues and repeat the "good" behaviors, your networks will become stronger, making the good behaviors more likely to become automatic.

You may also find it helpful to focus on retraining one bad habit at a time. Give it 30 days. And make sure to celebrate your successes—even the small ones—to help reinforce the new behavior.

The celebrations can be as simple as a fist pump, saying an "Attaboy" or "Attagirl" to yourself, or treating yourself to a new outfit in your new slimmer size. Whatever form the reward takes, your brain will remember that celebration and start associating it with the good behavior!

CHAPTER 4

HOW TO CONQUER 10 COMMON BAD HABITS

NOW THAT YOU KNOW the five steps to conquering your worst habits, let's take a look at 10 of the most common bad habits people come to me about and see what those steps look like in action.

Bad Habit #1: Saying Yes When You Should Say No

This people-pleasing bad habit overwhelms people and can make them bitter and chronically stressed. Like many bad habits, it is associated with low prefrontal cortex activity, which limits forethought. When someone asks you to do something, you reflexively say yes without thinking through all the consequences and end up so busy you don't have time for family and other priorities.

Most people say yes when they should say no because they erroneously believe that if they do more for people, those people will approve of and like them more.

I once treated Carter, an attorney who told me he didn't have time to work out or eat healthy because he was so busy. When we went through his week, it was clear he had committed himself to many activities that served other people's needs but few of his own.

I taught him the magic phrase "I have to think about it," and I had him practice saying it over and over in front of the mirror. Then I told him to filter every request for his time through this question: Does this fit the goals I have for my life? And when I said that, I was referring to the goals we talked about in the previous chapter on the One Page Miracle (i.e., relational goals, work goals, financial goals, and the goals he set for his physical, emotional, or spiritual health). If it didn't meet any of his goals, we decided that he would politely decline.

Over three months, this simple exercise changed his life. He had more time for his wife and children, for sleep, and even for some pro bono work (which was one of his goals).

How to Stop Saying Yes When You Should Say No

1. *Identify the bad habit and start tracking it.* Do you often feel overwhelmed, tired, or as though you have no time for yourself? Then you probably have a problem over-committing yourself. Start taking a mental note of all the requests for help that come your way.
2. *Ask yourself, What are the cues or triggers?* The phrases "Would you mind . . . ?" "If you have time . . ." "I was wondering . . ." or "Could you please do me a favor?"
3. *Identify the rewards you get from this behavior.* Mostly immediate (e.g., being the good guy or gal, being liked).
4. *Identify other or better benefits that you could get, were it not for this behavior.*

Time for things that matter more to you and better mental health.

5. *Build a new routine.* Whenever someone asks you to do something, start by saying, "I have to think about it." Then filter your response through the goals you have (again, check your One Page Miracle). If it doesn't fit, politely decline, but be firm by saying something like "I'm not going to be able to fit that into my schedule." You might even want to write "I have to think about it" on some Post-it Notes and stick them in at least three places you see daily. (Hint: Try placing them near objects you typically see when you get asked for favors, e.g., by or on your calendar, by or on your computer).

Remember, it takes time to rewire your brain, so—as I experienced with the bread—saying no might not come easily at first, but if you stick to the five-step plan, you *will* reap the benefits!

Bad Habit #2: Automatically Saying No or Arguing

This is the opposite of the previous bad habit. I sometimes liken it to "the terrible twos." It is normal for two-year-old children to assert their independence and automatically say no. That's why whenever I wanted a kiss from one of my kids when they were 2, I'd use reverse psychology and say I *didn't* want a kiss, which generally worked (don't judge me for being manipulative). Children usually outgrow the automatic "no" between the ages of 3 and 4. It's cute when they're 2, but it's really irritating when they're 6, 16, 46, or 86.

Many years ago, I noticed that people who tended to be argumentative or oppositional (automatically say no) had increased activity in the anterior cingulate gyrus (ACG) in the frontal lobes. The ACG is the brain's gear shifter. It is involved with cognitive flexibility, as well as shifting attention, seeing options, and detecting errors. When it works too hard, people worry (or fixate on certain thoughts), are rigid or inflexible, hold grudges, see too many errors in themselves and others, and often get stuck on the words and phrases *no*, *no way*, *never*, and *you can't make me do it*. (See why I call it the terrible twos?)

My dad had this bad habit. Whenever I'd ask him for something, such as permission to borrow the car, the answer was automatically, "No." My siblings and I knew if we wanted something from Dad, he would first say no, but then a week or two later, after thinking about the request, sometimes he'd change his mind. But "No" was always his first response.

In 1972, when I turned 18, I had to sign up for the draft because the US was still at war in Vietnam. When I showed interest in joining the Army to become a veterinarian's assistant (I had wanted to become a veterinarian since I was young), my father told me I couldn't do it (his automatic response) because there was a war going on. So what did I do? I joined the Army! Three weeks later, I was in basic training at Fort Ord, outside Monterey, California, with my head shaved and people screaming at me, calling me a maggot. Because my dad said I couldn't do it, I had to do it (a normal adolescent process called individuation). If he had said, "That's an interesting idea; let's talk about it," it's likely I would have never been called a maggot.

How to Stop Automatically Saying No or Arguing

1. *Track it.* If your first response is no, or you start formulating an argument in your head before people have even finished their comments, you likely have this habit. And don't automatically say you don't have it—a natural tendency.
2. *What are the cues or triggers?* Whenever someone asks you for something or to do something, or when you are in an emotional conversation.
3. *Identify the rewards you get from this behavior.* Immediate: being right, staying in control, having sovereignty over your time and decisions.
4. *Identify other or better benefits that you could get were it not for this behavior.* Long-term: improved cooperation and relationships with family, friends, and coworkers.
5. *Build a new routine.* Before answering questions or responding to requests in a

> negative way, catch yourself. Often it's helpful to take a deep breath, just to get extra time before responding. For example, if your spouse asks you to do something, before you say no, take a deep breath and ask yourself if saying no is *really* in everyone's best interest, and/or if it fits the goals you have for the relationship. (Once again, check the goals on your One Page Miracle.) In fact, you can use the same line that I gave for the previous bad habit: "I have to think about it."

Make a new habit of recognizing the automatic tendency to argue or say no, and take a deep breath to pause and ask yourself what response is really in the best interest of the situation and relationship. Then you'll be able to stop the automatic no from ruining or putting unnecessary strain on your relationships.

Bad Habit #3: Interrupting

Watch any political talk show and you'll see and hear people screaming and talking over each other. They don't really listen; they just say the first thing that comes to mind. As soon as someone else says something, the other person is already formulating a response without really even knowing what the other person is saying. Political pundits do this. Supervisors do this. Many parents do this—and it shuts down communication.

Over the years, many patients have told me that they are brutally honest. That's usually not helpful. In lectures, I often ask audiences, "How many of you are married?" Half the audience will raise their hands. Then I ask, "Is it helpful for you to say everything you think in your marriage?" The audience laughs and collectively says, "No!"

People with this habit can be rude, justify their behavior by saying they have to speak up or they'll forget what they were going to say, and tend to dominate conversations. In addition, people with this habit have trouble waiting in lines. Children and employees often clam up when a parent or supervisor suffers from this bad habit.

People who interrupt others usually have low activity in their prefrontal cortex, so they don't filter what they're going to say before they say it. Thinking about the impact your words will have on others before you say them is critical to healthy relationships.

Over the years, I've seen many teenagers who were shut down because their parents talked over them, didn't listen, and were constantly telling the teens how to think. That's what happened to Brandon. At 15, he became depressed and rebelled. As soon as he got home from school, he would shut himself in his room and come out only to grab some food. If his parents tried to coax him out of his room, he would lash out, telling them to leave him alone. His parents thought Brandon was the problem and brought him to see me. They told me he was uncommunicative and guaranteed that he wouldn't talk to me. I told the parents to leave Brandon with me.

When it was just the two of us, I let him know that I was there to listen to him, and I gave him the space he needed to express himself. Over time, he opened up and told me that his parents never allowed him to finish a sentence or to share his opinions, so he just gave up trying. That's when I invited his parents to become a part of Brandon's therapy and helped them understand that they were part of the problem and could be part of the solution.

How to Stop Interrupting

1. *Track it.* Has anyone told you that you interrupt or jump into conversations too quickly? Do people tend to shut down around you? Do you tend to say the first thing that comes to mind without considering the impact your words have on others before you say them, or do you tend to act without thinking? These are all clues that you have a problem with interrupting people. Start paying attention to it.
2. *What are the cues or triggers?* Triggers worth paying attention to might be conversations with people close to you, such as coworkers and friends; when you are intoxicated (by the way, stop drinking), hungry, tired, angry, in an argument, or overwhelmed by your partner's words.
3. *Identify the rewards you get from this behavior.* Immediate: venting or blowing

off steam, relieving stress, getting your point across, feeling the need to be right.

4. *Identify other or better benefits that you could get were it not for this behavior.* Better long-term connections, more input, and better relationships.
5. *Build a new routine.* There are two antidotes to interrupting that improve communication and overall relationship health: learning to ask, "Then what?" and active listening.

Before you say something, filter it through the impact it may have on others. I often teach my patients to ask themselves, "If I say this, or if I do this, then what are the consequences? Will it bring me closer to my spouse, improve my relationship with my boss, help my children develop in a responsible way, improve my own health?" The more you filter your words and deeds through what you really want, the less "brutally honest" you will be.

Active listening dramatically improves communication. In fact, most psychotherapists teach this skill. It is simple and goes like this:

Step 1: Listen and do not interrupt, no matter how much you get the urge.

Step 2: Repeat back what you hear: "I hear you saying . . ."

Step 3: Listen for the feelings behind what you're hearing: "Sounds like you are feeling frustrated."

Step 4: Listen to the person's response carefully and reflect it back again.

Active listening forces you to pay attention and stops you from thinking about what you're going to say next so you can hear the other person. The rewards are that it increases communication, immediately clears up misunderstandings, and cools down conflicts. When people feel heard, they can often talk through and solve their own problems. When people don't feel heard, or when someone talks over them, it can trigger feelings of abandonment, invisibility, insignificance, or anger. Active listening can miraculously change relationships in a short period of time.

Bad Habit #4: Lying

This is a sneaky habit. Lying leads to mistrust in your relationships, and if you can lie to others, you also lie to yourself. Of course, you do not need to be brutally honest. I often tell my patients there are ways to say things and there are *more tactful* ways to say things. And yet, lying is a very common bad habit. In fact, according to one study, most people lie once or twice a day.[1] People lie for many different reasons, including

- to avoid being punished
- to protect oneself
- to avoid disappointing others
- to avoid embarrassment
- to obtain a reward they did not earn
- to promote oneself
- to protect another person from being punished
- to get out of an uncomfortable social situation
- to exercise power over others

Lying can even ruin your health. One study found that 81 percent of patients lie to their doctors in at least one of seven scenarios: not adhering to prescription medication as instructed, not exercising regularly or at all, not understanding a doctor's instructions, disagreeing with a doctor's recommendations, maintaining an unhealthy diet, taking a specific medication, or taking someone else's medication.[2] It's nearly impossible for you to get the help you need if you're not honest with your caregivers.

There is a difference between "normal" liars—those of us who tell harmless little white lies—and pathological liars.

NORMAL LIARS

- give compliments that are not 100 percent genuine
- tell people they're doing well, when they really aren't
- say they are busy to avoid others

PATHOLOGICAL LIARS

- lie habitually, even when there is no clear benefit

- lie to make themselves look like the hero or victim, and the stories they tell are dramatic, complicated, and detailed
- get a thrill from getting away with it
- tell more lies per day than a normal liar tells
- tend to be younger, male, and have higher occupational status—bad news for hedge fund managers, attorneys, and doctors
- lie the most to their partners and children
- believe lying is acceptable and are not deterred by guilt or risk of exposure
- are more likely to lie for their own self-interest, such as to protect a secret

Even children lie. As a child psychiatrist, I've been teaching parent training for many years. One of the first steps in the program is to have parents post a few rules at home to guide and direct behavior. Rule number one is "Tell the truth." The rule is very clear: Tell the truth! This includes little lies and big ones. I've found that when you allow a child to get away with the little lies, the bigger ones will come more easily.

As a parent, one of the best gifts you can give your children is to teach them to be honest, which builds trust in relationships. Plus, if they can be honest with others, they are more likely to be honest with themselves. So when they tell a lie to get out of trouble, see that they get a consequence for the wrong act and another one for lying.

Of course, if you want children to follow this rule, you cannot tell lies either. Remember, children do what you do, not what you *tell* them to do. So, when someone calls and you do not want to talk, telling your child to lie for you and say you aren't home is not okay because it teaches your child that lying *is* okay.

When lying becomes a chronic problem, I teach parents an exercise called Truth Training, which begins by identifying lying as a problem to be solved, rather than an indictment on the child's character. For example, when I told my mother a lie at age 6, she cried and told me she never thought she would have a child who would go to hell. Don't do that! Simply tell the child why lying is a problem—i.e., people will not trust them—and tell them you are going to ask them questions you already know the answer to. If they answer honestly, you will be very happy and give them a small reward, such as extra time together, and if they lie, there will be a consequence, such as extra chores. Do it in a matter-of-fact way, without emotion, and always root for them to tell the truth.

How to Stop Lying

1. *Track it.* Track how many times you lie today and in a typical week.
2. *What are the cues or triggers?* When you feel trapped, when you don't want to hurt someone's feelings, or when you hate the truth.
3. *Identify the rewards you get for this behavior.* Immediate: (depending on the reason for the lie) avoid being punished, protect oneself, avoid disappointing others, avoid embarrassment, obtain a reward you did not earn, promote oneself, protect another person from being punished, get out of an uncomfortable social situation, or exercise power over others.

4. *Identify other or better benefits that you could get were it not for this behavior.* Long-term: feel better about yourself, remember facts more clearly, less stress.
5. *Build a new routine.* When you catch yourself starting to lie, take a breath, pause and say, "I meant . . ." followed by the truth. Journal your lies to stay aware of them. Your self-esteem will go up when your lies go down. And please, immediately stop lying to your health-care professionals. I often tell my patients their number one job in healing is to tell me the truth; otherwise, we are wasting everyone's time and their money.

I'd be lying if I said lying is an easy habit to break, but if you commit to changing your behavior, you *can* do it.

Bad Habit #5: Becoming Easily Distracted

Smartphones, laptops, tablets, email, text messages, the internet, and streaming services are stealing our time and attention. In fact, many people are not only watching TV, but they are also on other devices at the same time. And technology companies are constantly creating newer and better addictive gadgets to hook our attention and distract us from meaningful relationships. Case in point: Many people are on their phones at mealtimes rather than interacting with family members.

Even more concerning, technology is hijacking still-developing brains with potentially serious consequences for many. In fact, a 2015 study found that teens actually spend more time on entertainment media (average nine hours) than they do asleep; tweens are online six hours a day.[3] And as video-game and technology usage go up, so do obesity and depression.[4] Ian Bogost, famed video-game designer (*Cow Clicker* and *Cruel 2 B Kind*) and professor and director of film and media studies and professor of computer science and engineering at Washington University in St. Louis, calls the wave of new habit-forming technologies "the cigarette of this century" and warns of their equally addictive and potentially destructive side effects.[5]

In 2015, disturbing research from Microsoft reported that humans lose concentration after about eight seconds, while the lowly goldfish loses its focus after about nine seconds.[6] It seems like evolution may be going in the wrong direction. In 2000, the human attention span average was estimated at 12 seconds, which is not great; but losing a third of our attention span in 15 years is alarming![7]

And according to an article in the *Harvard Business Review*, "Beware the Busy Manager,"[8] our unhealthy lifestyles are diminishing our capacity at work. Only 10 percent of managers are high in both focus and energy, two of the main ingredients for success. The authors found that 20 percent were disengaged, 30 percent were high in procrastination, and 40 percent were easily distracted. This means that 90 percent of managers, and likely the rest of us, lack focus and/or energy (see chart that follows).

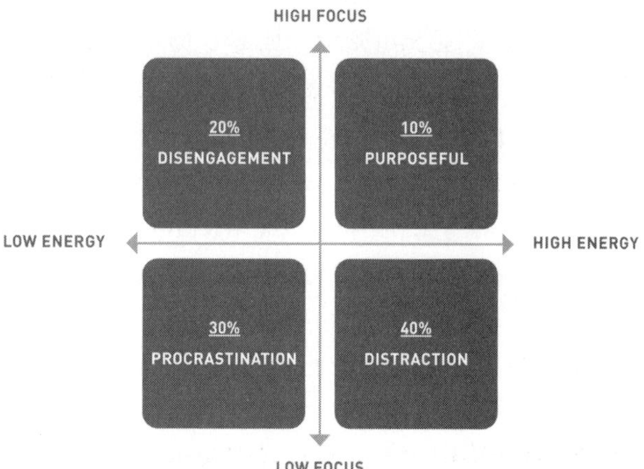

How to Focus

1. *Track it.* Take note of how many times an hour you become distracted. (And yes, I realize this may be difficult.)
2. *What are the cues or triggers?* Being bombarded by phone calls, emails, texts, etc.
3. *Identify the rewards you get from this behavior.* Immediate: satisfy the addiction of having to know what's next; avoid facing or dealing with problems.
4. *Identify other or better benefits that you could get were it not for this behavior.*

Long-term: more time, less stress, better focus.

5. *Build a new routine.* When you need to get things done, shut down your email and put your phone on airplane mode. Your productivity will go way up. Try AppDetox to help stop your phone from distracting you.

Still with me? Good! On to the next bad habit.

Bad Habit #6: Procrastinating

Procrastination is the act of unnecessarily postponing decisions or actions. When you wait until the very last minute to get things done (completing schoolwork, paperwork, or chores; paying bills; buying birthday, anniversary, or Christmas gifts; etc.), it increases stress and often irritates those around you who feel the need to pick up the loose pieces.

If it isn't the last minute, people who procrastinate cannot kick their brain into gear to get their work done. Many parents have told me about the constant fights they have with their children or teens about starting projects early and working on them over time, rather than beginning the night before. Many adults have told me they never did term papers in school, or they used amphetamines the night before a due date. Procrastination leads to poorly done, incomplete, or unfinished work.

Procrastination is a hallmark of ADD/ADHD, where your prefrontal cortex is not as strong as it could be. Procrastination is also associated with abstract goals, depression, perfectionism, never feeling as though you can get something just right, fear of failure, and low energy.

How to Stop Procrastinating

1. *Track it.* Start taking note of how many times a day you say or think, "I'll do it later" or I'll do it tomorrow." (And yes, I need you to start doing this today.)
2. *What are the cues or triggers?* You are faced with a task or a decision, but you would rather do something else.
3. *Identify the rewards you get from this behavior.* Immediate: don't have to expend energy and effort; can stay in the present moment; receive immediate gratification rather than future rewards.

4. *Identify other or better benefits you can get from changing this behavior.* Get more done with less stress and do a better job.
5. *Build a new routine.* As with lying, don't see procrastination as a character problem but rather as a problem to solve. The secret to stop procrastinating is to have a method to get things done. I use one that is just a few simple steps.

First, know what you want. The first things I look at each day are my One Page Miracle and my to-do and stop-doing lists. Don't try to do too many things at once or little will get done, which is why I also have a stop-doing list. Tim Cook, CEO of Apple, says, "We say no to good ideas every day. We do this to make great ideas happen."[9]

Second, have a one- to three-minute huddle with yourself at the beginning of every day. At Amen Clinics, one of our habits is a daily huddle, where the teams meet for a few minutes each morning to review what happened the day before and talk about what our goals are for the day, all in the context of our overall goals. The huddles keep us in a rhythm of getting things done. Having a brief huddle with yourself will significantly increase your productivity. Decide what you want to accomplish that day in the overall context of your life and write down three things you want to accomplish that day.

Third, do the most important things first. There's a reason dessert is at the end of the meal. If you eat it first, you won't get the nutrition you need. Stop eating dessert first with your time—get the most important tasks of the day done when your energy is highest.

Fourth, make sure you have everything you need to get the job done. Remember, achieving your goals is like trying to move a giant rock. It's not a question of effort but of having the right tools and a plan. For example, I schedule exercise rather than leave it up to "when I have time." If I schedule it, no one can take it from me. I also put my walking clothes out the night before so they are ready to go in the morning, and I wear a Fitbit to make sure I am constantly reminded to get enough exercise. Just putting on my watch nudges me to exercise.

Next, bundle things you love to do with things you tend to procrastinate about. For example, listen to podcasts or audiobooks while exercising, or watch your favorite television show while doing household chores. Most mornings, as I am walking, I'm also on a conference call with two of my work teams.

And finally, give yourself a reward. After you finish a difficult task, reward yourself with something special, such as a new book, a warm bath, or a cup of hot tea.

Bad Habit #7: Disorganization

Many people struggle with organization of both their time and their space. Often this is a direct result of other bad habits (saying yes when you should say no; becoming distracted; procrastinating). They tend to be late, finish tasks at the last moment, or have trouble completing tasks on time. They also tend to struggle keeping their spaces tidy, especially their rooms, book bags, filing cabinets, drawers, closets, and paperwork.

Psychiatrists say that people who are chronically unprepared for tasks or always late to appointments are often manifesting underlying hostility. They get their anger out in passive-aggressive ways; instead of telling someone they're mad, they act it out by being late or sabotaging their tasks.

Nothing is more frustrating to a boss, coworker, family member—anyone—than to be waiting on someone who is poorly organized, unprepared for their daily tasks, or late. You've probably felt the irritation of waiting for someone to finish a task later than planned or having to change plans because of somebody's poor organization.

If you're tired of being "that person" who is always frantic, late, and disheveled, you need to turn things around now—not just for your own benefit but to ease the frustration of those around you who suffer as a result.

How to Get Organized

1. *Track it.* Take a quick inventory of your room, desk, purse, closets, and drawers. Are they neat and tidy or kind of a mess? How often do you find yourself running late because you can't find something you need (like your glasses, shoes, phone, or car keys)?
2. *What are the cues or triggers?* Being in a hurry; not devoting time to organize your

day, tasks, or space; overloaded schedule; high stress; too many distractions.

3. *Identify the benefits of this behavior.* Immediate: You believe it saves you time.
4. *Identify other or better benefits of changing this behavior.* You will save much more time in the long run by being more organized and efficient.
5. *Build a new routine.* Ask for help from a friend or family member who is organized or hire a professional organizer to come to your home or work to teach you systems and to organize your spaces. Then make sure they come back monthly to hold you accountable and help you build the new habits.

Here are a few more organizational tips:

- Schedule similar tasks together, such as errands, appointments, maintenance, or phone calls.
- Keep a to-do list of the important tasks you need to get done today, this week, and in the near future. Update this list

as necessary. Relying on this list is more accurate than relying on your memory.

- Schedule your most important activities for the hours when you are at your peak.
- Learn to say no.
- Cut unwanted calls short. Unsolicited calls waste a lot of time. I often start conversations by saying something like "I only have a minute . . ." End calls that are taking too much time with something like "I have an appointment" (even if the appointment is only with yourself).
- Watch out for the great time thieves. These include procrastination, indecisiveness, regrets, fear of failure, worry, and distraction. Don't get distracted by low-value activities, such as social media, binge-watching series on Netflix, or playing video games.
- Be prepared for gifts of time. Always carry some work or relaxing things to do with you for times when you may have to wait, such as before doctors' appointments, in traffic jams, on an airplane, or on a commuter train. Use the time to your advantage

by listening to podcasts or audiobooks, writing notes or letters, creating a menu or grocery list, or tackling any other small task that's already on your to-do list. Change your perception of these moments from dead or wasted time to productive time.

Bad Habit #8: Chronic Pessimism

Do you know people who always think the sky is falling? Their minds habitually go to the worst possible outcome, and they express it to others. They frequently say negative things, or they constantly stir up trouble. I call this automatic tendency *chronic pessimism*. I first noticed it in one of my ADD/ADHD patients. She started every psychotherapy session by talking about how she was going to kill herself. She noticed this made me anxious and seemed to enjoy telling me the gruesome details of her plan. After about a year of listening to her, I finally realized she wasn't really going to kill herself. She was using my reaction as a source of stimulation. After getting to know her very well, I told her, "I don't think you want to kill yourself. You love your four children, and I can't believe you would ever abandon them or model suicide as a way for adults to handle problems. I think you use these stories as a way to stimulate your brain. You probably aren't aware of it, but your ADD/ADHD causes you to play the worst-case scenario game. This ruins any joy you could have in your life." (By the way, don't try this at home.)

Initially, she was very upset with me (another source of conflict, I told her), but she trusted me enough to at least look at the behavior. Decreasing this need for turmoil became one of our goals together and helped her over time.

I've noticed this bad habit in many other ADD/ADHD patients but also in those who have had concussions (injuring the prefrontal cortex), in people who didn't get much sleep (causing low blood flow to the prefrontal cortex), and in those who had undisciplined minds.

Without enough stimulation to the prefrontal cortex, the brain looks for ways to increase its own activity. Being upset, angry, or negative acts as a stimulant that increases the fight-or-flight neurotransmitter adrenaline, which increases your heart rate, blood pressure, and muscle tension, just as a cup of coffee or a bit of cocaine does.

People with chronic pessimism tend to pick on others to get a rise out of them or make them upset. It is unconscious behavior, and they are often not aware they are doing it. I've heard many times from parents of ADD/ADHD children, "If we have a bad morning at home, our child has a good day at school" (the yelling and fighting stimulated them), or "If we have a good morning at home, he had a bad day at school" (there was no stimulation, so the child picked on other kids or the teacher). So often, family members of my patients say, "I'm so tired of fighting with my brother [sister, mother, father, son, daughter, etc.]. Why does there have to be this turmoil? It seems as if they cannot be happy with peaceful coexistence. They have to fight."

If this sounds like you or someone close to you, chronic pessimism may be the culprit.

How to Stop Chronic Pessimism

1. *Track it.* Do you tend to find the negative wherever you look or stir up trouble for no particular reason? When people give you a compliment, do you find a way to diminish it? When someone says, "You

look nice today," is your go-to response, "Didn't I look nice yesterday?" If someone at work says, "We had really great sales this month," do you immediately ask, "What happened *last* month?" When your teen comes home and says, "I got all A's and one B," do you celebrate the A's with them, or ask, "What's with the B?" If this sounds like you, start paying special attention to how you receive and respond to comments and compliments.

2. *What are the cues or triggers?* Being around people you envy. Not feeling good about yourself or feeling self-conscious. Feeling like you're not pulling your weight at work or at home. Feeling bored.
3. *Identify the benefits of this behavior.* Immediate: Some people feel better when they make others feel worse—to even out the field, so to speak. Others feel like pointing out someone else's flaws distracts from their own.
4. *Identify other or better benefits of changing this behavior.* In addition to improving your relationships, eliminating pessimism

can also improve your mental health, provide a boost to your immune system, and help prevent chronic disease. Now that's something to be happy about!

5. *Build a new routine.* The next time you are tempted to say something negative, take a beat and ask yourself, "Is what I'm about to say helpful or hurtful to the other person/this situation?" before you speak and adjust your reply accordingly. And the next time someone compliments you, instead of questioning it, simply say, "Thank you," and say something kind in return.

Remember the Golden Rule. Treat others the way you would like to be treated, and make a habit of being the type of person *you* would want to spend time with.

Bad Habit #9: Overeating

Nearly everywhere you go (schools, work, shopping malls, movie theaters, airports, ballparks, etc.), someone is trying to sell you food that will kill you early and that feeds your bad habit. The

Standard American Diet (SAD) is filled with pro-inflammatory foods that increase your risk for diabetes, hypertension, heart disease, cancer, ADD/ADHD, depression, dementia, and obesity, which is now a serious national crisis with 73 percent of Americans overweight and 40 percent obese.[10]

Food manufacturing corporations don't even try to hide the fact that they purposely make their junk foods addictive. Just think of that Lay's Potato Chips advertising campaign that proudly claimed, "Betcha can't eat just one!"[11] They were right. Junk food giants rely on food scientists to expertly engineer snack items with just the right amounts of unhealthy ingredients to create the perfect combination of flavors and texture to overwhelm the brain to its "bliss point." It's like a hit of cocaine, which activates the brain's reward system and makes you want more, more, more! This is one of the reasons people say they love ice cream, chips, cake, and french fries, and they can't imagine giving them up.

And the excessive fat these foods put on your body is not innocuous. It disrupts your hormones, stores toxins, and produces chemicals that increase inflammation.[12] When obesity is combined with diabetes, which I call "diabesity," the risk is worse. High blood sugar levels damage your blood vessels.[13]

Our weight problem is not just an adult issue. In children ages 2 to 19, obesity increased from 13.9 percent in 1999–2000 to 18.5 percent in 2015–2016.[14] Food scientists and fast food companies are targeting your kids with weapons of mass destruction, which I define as foods that are highly processed, pesticide sprayed, artificially colored and sweetened, high in sugars, low in fiber, food-like but not real, laden with hormones, and tainted with antibiotics.

Excess fat on your body is not your friend. Obesity is detrimental to brain health/mental health and is associated with a greater risk of depression, bipolar disorder, panic disorder, agoraphobia (fear of going out), and addictions.[15] Untreated attention deficit disorder/attention deficit hyperactivity disorder (ADD/ADHD),[16] lower self-esteem, and poor body image[17] are also associated with being overweight.[18] Among women, increased body mass index (BMI) is also linked to a rise in suicidal thoughts.[19] Being overweight or obese has also been associated with a smaller brain and decreased blood flow to the brain.[20] It also makes you more susceptible to developing sleep problems, such as sleep apnea.[21]

I've been writing and teaching about this for decades now. Many published studies, including two of my own, report that as your weight goes up, the size and function of your brain go down.

Don't let this bad habit hijack your brain and your relationships. It'll ruin your health and invite a host of other bad habits to the party.

How to Stop Overeating

1. *Track it.* For the next few days, keep a food log of everything you eat both during and between meals.
2. *What are the cues or triggers?* Pay attention to your most vulnerable times. When do you find yourself craving snacks? Morning, lunch, midafternoon, dinnertime, late night? Many people who overeat at night are not hungry in the morning. Location also matters. Whenever I go to a movie theater and smell the pro-inflammatory popcorn

raised with pesticides and cooked in unhealthy oils, the smell triggers the desire for it, even though I know better. Likewise, for some strange reason, whenever I pass a Jack-in-the-Box, my brain wants an iced tea and a chicken fajita sandwich, which is not the worst thing in the world, but it's certainly not the best.

Being with specific people or at specific places can also trigger cravings—especially if you tend to eat certain foods or get drinks with them. For me, my mom's house was one of them. When I made the decision to get healthy, I would eat something healthy before I went to her home, so my overeating was under control.

Many people also use food to change their moods. Carbohydrate-laden foods boost serotonin and help calm the brain's emotional centers, which is why people get addicted to doughnuts, cupcakes, cookies, and bread.

3. *Identify the rewards you get from this behavior.* Immediate: satisfy cravings.

4. *Identify other or better benefits from eliminating this behavior.* Long-term: leaner, smarter, happier, healthier, and longer life.
5. *Build a new routine.* Your brain already has a food routine—is it serving you or hurting you? If it is not serving you, create a new one. Here's mine:

   » Breakfast: either eggs and organic blueberries or a healthy shake around 10 a.m. (I do 12 to 16 hours of intermittent fasting most days.)
   » Snack: fresh-cut veggies with mashed avocados or an apple and almonds
   » Lunch: salad with grilled veggies and a protein, such as chicken or lamb
   » Afternoon snack: nuts and fruit
   » Dinner: protein and veggies
   » Dessert: sugar-free dark chocolate or fruit

The trick is to find foods you love that love you back and schedule them into your meals.

Make a list of foods you like that fit within the following six simple brain-healthy rules for eating:

- Eat high-quality calories and not too many of them. I think of calories like money. Overspend and your health will become bankrupt.
- Eat clean protein at every meal to balance your blood sugar and decrease cravings.
- Focus your diet on healthy fats from fish, nuts, seeds, and avocados. Fat is essential for brain health.
- When you feel hungry, first drink a glass of water to make sure you were not really thirsty.
- Eat smart carbohydrates that do not raise your blood sugar, such as those found in colorful fruits and vegetables, and limit sugar and carbs that quickly turn to sugar, such as bread, pasta, potatoes, and rice. I call these dumb carbs because they're pro-inflammatory, and studies show they can decrease IQ.

- Liberally use brain-healthy spices, especially pepper, cinnamon, nutmeg, garlic, cloves, and turmeric.

To fend off cravings, focus on the biology of decision-making: Know what you want (to be at a healthy weight), keep your blood sugar stable (eat small portions of protein and healthy fat at each meal), make sure to get seven to eight hours of sleep at night, limit alcohol, and limit low-quality foods that quickly turn to sugar, such as bread, pasta, potatoes, rice, and sugar. Planning your food is critical. The payoff is that your prefrontal cortex gets stronger and healthier at the same time. Your decision-making improves, and you start taking control of your life.

Bad Habit #10: Not Thinking Before You Act

I start many of my lectures with a terrifying video of two women who became trapped on an 80-foot-high railroad bridge with a freight train barreling toward them. Obviously, the train surprised them as they walked along the tracks. Ultimately, the women survived by lying down flat in the middle of the tracks. I show the video because it reminds me of how blind most people are to the health of their brains. If you knew brain-health troubles were coming, would you get out of the way? Or would you be like these two women, oblivious to the pitfalls of walking on a railway bridge with no escape?

Every single day, we are exposed to a host of chemicals, pesticides, fumes, and products that poison the human brain. Common toxins in the air we breathe, the foods we eat, and the products we rub on our skin are absorbed into our bodies via our lungs, digestive system, and pores, and can eventually impact the brain. The more exposure we have to these everyday toxins, the more we are putting our brains at risk and increasing our chances of brain health/mental health issues.

Your brain is the most metabolically active organ in your body. Even though it is only 2 percent of your body's weight, it uses 20 to 30 percent of the calories you consume and 20 percent of the blood flow and oxygen.[22] Exposure to any dangerous substance can damage your brain and your life.

Not thinking before you act (overeating, putting toxic products on your body, never thinking about the health of your brain and body) is likely the worst of all the bad habits. This is what happens when you let your brain run on autopilot. In this case, your brain is not listening to what it needs to stay healthy.

This bad habit is killing us as a society—rates of hypertension, diabesity (diabetes + obesity), depression, and obesity are skyrocketing, and so are the costs! Seventy-five percent of health-care dollars in the United States are spent on chronic, preventable illnesses.[23]

I write extensively about healthy habits that can improve your brain function and general overall health in my book *The End of Mental Illness*, but for now, let's focus on getting into the habit of actively asking yourself, "Is what I'm about to do, eat, drink, or engage in good for my brain (and body) or bad for it?"

How to Start Paying Attention to Your Health

1. *Track it.* Dangerous toxins are all around us every day. Over the years, our clinic has developed a checklist to help patients determine how much contact they may

have had with harmful substances. By answering the questions below, you can begin to determine your own risk—and begin taking steps to combat that exposure.

- ☐ Do you smoke, or are you around secondhand smoke?
- ☐ Do you smoke marijuana?
- ☐ Do you use conventional cleaning products and inadvertently breathe the fumes?
- ☐ Have you been exposed to carbon monoxide?
- ☐ Do you travel on planes more than six times a year?
- ☐ Do you pump your own gas or breathe automobile exhaust?
- ☐ Do you live in an area with moderate to high air pollution?[24]
- ☐ Have you lived or worked in a building that had water damage and mold in it?
- ☐ Do you come in contact with flame-resistant clothing or carpet, or with

furnishings sprayed with chemicals to prevent stains?

- ☐ Do you spray your garden, farm, or orchard with pesticides or live near an area with pesticides?[25]
- ☐ Do you paint indoors without ventilation?
- ☐ Do you have more than four glasses of alcohol a week?
- ☐ Do you regularly eat processed or fast foods?
- ☐ Do you regularly eat conventionally raised produce, meat, or dairy, or farm-raised fish?
- ☐ Do you eat large (i.e., mercury-contaminated) fish, such as swordfish?
- ☐ Do you eat nonorganic fruits and vegetables on a regular basis?
- ☐ Do you consume foods with artificial colors or sweeteners, such as diet sodas, or use artificial sweeteners, such as aspartame (NutraSweet), sucralose (Splenda), or saccharin (Sweet'N Low)?
- ☐ Do you use more than two health and/or beauty products per day?

(Most people never read the labels or understand how many chemicals are included.)

- ☐ Do you live in a house that contains lead pipes or copper plumbing soldered with lead (built prior to 1978)?
- ☐ Do you wear lipstick or kiss someone with lipstick made with lead? (Sixty percent of the lipstick sold in the United States has lead in it.[26])
- ☐ Do you have mercury amalgam fillings? How many?
- ☐ Do you work in a job where you are exposed to environmental toxins, such as firefighter, painter, welder, or dockworker?

2. *What are the cues or triggers?* Almost any decision in your day. Literally everything we ingest or come into contact with can have an impact on our health.
3. *Identify the rewards you get from this behavior.* Immediate: Being oblivious to how the decisions we make every day impact our health is easy and doesn't require any thinking.

4. *Identify other or better benefits of changing this behavior.* Long-term: better mental and physical health, more energy, and longevity. The benefits of actively taking care of your brain and body are virtually endless.
5. *Build a new routine.* Before you buy anything, eat anything, drink anything, do anything, or say anything, ask yourself, "Is this good for my brain or bad for it?" Repeat it over and over until this question becomes a habit itself. Start getting serious about being well and learn what's good for you and your brain. See my book *The End of Mental Illness* for an extensive list of ways to prevent or treat the risk factors that hurt your brain and for simple strategies to boost overall brain health.

Next Steps

Hopefully by now you have a solid grasp on how the five steps, in conjunction with the One Page Miracle, can help you overcome most—if not all—of your worst and most annoying bad habits.

Unfortunately, in some cases—especially when there are toxic substances like drugs or alcohol involved—the five steps aren't enough. In our next chapter, we're going to look at what happens when bad habits become addictions and outline some of the ways you, or someone you love, can get help.

CHAPTER 5

WHEN BAD HABITS BECOME ADDICTIONS

WHEN BAD HABITS GET OUT OF CONTROL or your prefrontal cortex is weak, you may become vulnerable to addictions. And increased stress—at home, school, or work—can make you even more susceptible to addiction.

The good news is that while plenty of people will abuse substances or engage in addictive behaviors and suffer consequences, they often stop when they see the devastation their behavior causes, like these patients I have treated over the years:

Leslie, 23, had too much to drink at her company holiday party and came on to her boss . . .

in front of his wife! She was fired the next day at work. Leslie felt humiliated and vowed never to get that drunk again. And she didn't.

Derek, 16, was on the soccer team in high school. One day, he and his soccer teammates found a peephole to the girls' locker room where they saw the girls changing out of their clothes. A girl passing by outside noticed the group of guys, realized what they were doing, and turned them in to the school principal. Derek and his buddies got suspended for a week, and Derek never looked through a peephole again.

Tracy, 44, was so anxious about what she was seeing in the news that she went to the store and filled her cart with cupcakes, cheesecake, fudge brownies, and chocolate-covered pretzels. When she came home, she tore into the packages and stuffed them in her mouth. Within minutes of finishing her umpteen-thousand-calorie feast, she felt sick to her stomach. She spent most of the night throwing up, and the next day, she still felt queasy. She swore off bingeing and went back to her normal eating routine.

Unfortunately, some people will abuse substances or engage in self-destructive behaviors, have adverse consequences, and then continue their addictive choices despite the trouble they are causing, like some of my other patients:

Robbie, 25, went to his company's holiday party and got so trashed he went up to his supervisor and insulted her with a vulgar term in front of the company CEO. Robbie was fired on the spot. The next night, he went out to a bar with a friend to "celebrate" the fact that he didn't have to work with that "nasty woman" anymore. He got drunk again and was charged with a DUI as he drove home.

Brandon, 49, was only 14 years old when he peered through an open window to sneak a peek at his sister coming out of the shower. He felt an incredible rush, but his sister caught him in the act, told their parents, and got Brandon into big trouble. The next day, all Brandon could think about was the strong arousal he felt from watching her, so later that day, he peered through his sister's bedroom window to watch her change clothes. He got caught again, and his parents grounded him for a month. Years later, Brandon placed a hidden camera in the bathroom of an apartment he was renting out so he could watch his female tenant in the shower. She found the camera and sued Brandon for $1 million—even that didn't stop his voyeurism.

Stacey, 36, started bingeing 20 years ago when she got cut from the high school drill team. She went home and ate everything she could find in the kitchen cupboards. The sickness that followed didn't deter her from doing it again when her boyfriend dumped her, when she didn't get into her first-choice college, or when she didn't land the job she wanted. Even the fact that she had gained 30 pounds and hated the way she looked couldn't keep her from bingeing whenever something bad or stressful happened in her life.

What's the difference between those who overdo it with alcohol, food, sex, or other addictive behaviors but learn from their mistakes and those who minimize the consequences and continue in the same destructive behaviors over and over?

For the latter group, past trauma (neglect, abuse, codependence, etc.), negative outside influences (parents, coaches, bosses, coworkers, bullies, etc.), and subtle manipulation (especially from the media and advertisers), along with a weak prefrontal cortex, overwhelm them to such a degree that addiction simply takes over. And when that happens, it's time to get help.

The Missing Link

Let me start by saying that I'm a fan of Alcoholics Anonymous and other 12-step programs. I have seen AA, along with Narcotics Anonymous (NA), Cocaine Anonymous (CA), Overeaters Anonymous (OA), and similar programs change people's lives, including the lives of my own family members.

Powerful and time-tested, anonymous programs have worked for millions of people around the world. Yet they clearly do not work for everyone. In fact, a study conducted by the Department of Veterans Affairs showed 43 percent of attendees were sober at 18 months.[1]

One of the reasons for the lower efficacy is that this program and many other recovery programs include no steps to address the physical functioning of the brain, which is the missing link to breaking any addiction.

Your brain is involved in everything you do and everything you are. Simply put, when your brain works right, you work right, but when it is troubled for any reason, you are much more likely to have trouble in your life—especially when it comes to addictions. You can diligently work all the anonymous steps (AA, NA, CA, etc.) with energy, enthusiasm, and commitment, but if your brain is not working at an optimal level (and most brains aren't), you will have a much harder time getting and staying sober, despite your best efforts.

With this in mind, let me offer 12 new steps to breaking the chains of addiction.

Step 1: Know What You Want

Most addiction-recovery programs start with acknowledging trouble, by knowing when you are powerless over a substance or behavior. You should start one step earlier by knowing exactly what you want in life. Remember, if you tell your brain what you want, it can help make it happen.

In the addiction world, therapists will often ask clients if they have a high bottom (you learn quickly) or a low bottom (you have to lose everything before you get help). When I was 16, I got drunk on a six-pack of Michelob and a half bottle of champagne. I was sick for three days and have had very little alcohol since then. I often wonder why other people think it's fun. For me, it wasn't, plus I acted like a fool, which was embarrassing. So, I have a high bottom. Actor Chris Browning, star of *Bosch*, *Westworld*, and *Sons of Anarchy*, joined us in 2020 on our podcast *The Brain Warrior's Way* (now called the *Change Your Brain Every Day* podcast). He told my wife, Tana, and me that he had used heroin for six years. He went from having a beachfront home in Malibu to being homeless under the 405 Freeway and was arrested multiple times before he finally got sober. He has a low bottom.

No one starts out wanting to have a low bottom. But addiction makes it easy to lose sight of what's most important to you. Take, for example, the late Jerry Garcia.

My friend Dr. David Smith, founder of the famous Haight Ashbury Free Clinic in San Francisco, once told me a story about attending a medical conference in Chicago in 1989 when he got a frantic call from Bill Graham, the legendary rock concert promoter. Graham was on tour with the Grateful Dead and told David, "Jerry Garcia is strung out, and you have to do something." David headed to the band's hotel, where he had to snake his way through a sea of tie-dye-clad groupies and billows of marijuana smoke to get to Garcia's room. Inside, he was welcomed by Graham and Garcia's bandmates: bass player Phil Lesh and rhythm guitarist Bob Weir, who was in recovery from hard drugs.

Drugs and rock and roll had been a way of life for Garcia for decades. While on tour with the Dead, people would give him all the drugs he wanted. He would often smoke heroin backstage just to make himself feel better. The years of hard partying and touring had not been kind to Garcia. He was severely overweight, had diabetes, and had even slipped into a diabetic coma a few years earlier. But that wasn't enough to make him want to change his ways.

The band told Garcia that he was killing himself with drugs, and they were staging an intervention. It wasn't the first intervention they had tried. Garcia had run away from the last one and subsequently gotten arrested for possession. This time, though, his bandmates told him that they would no longer go out on the road with him unless he got help for his addiction. For Garcia, touring with the band and playing music for thousands of people was what he loved most in life. The threat of losing that is what finally motivated him to change and enter a holistic addiction treatment center.

Step 2: Know When Your Addiction Has Taken You Hostage

This step is similar to Step 1 in the AA model—know when you are powerless and your life is unmanageable. So how do you know when you are in trouble? Many people are in denial about their behavior and are very slow to admit when they have a problem. I often tell my patients the answer is simple: You're an addict when your behavior (drinking, drugs, eating, shopping, gambling, sex, etc.) gets you into trouble with your relationships, health, work, money, or the law—and you do it again. You don't learn that the behavior gets you into trouble, or you cannot stop it.

For many people, problem behaviors creep up slowly, and the changes are hard to notice. By the time you are firmly in the grasp of addiction, your brain has rewired itself and it drives you to continue the addiction in spite of the consequences.

Addictions can impact every aspect of your life, including your physical, mental, and emotional health; social life; and core values. They can also fuel other problems, which can be biological, psychological, social, or spiritual. Most people with an addiction will exhibit issues in several if not all of these areas.

Here is an example:

Cole was a shy, quiet 16-year-old who loved playing the piano and being in the math club. When one of his older brother's friends introduced him to cocaine, he immediately loved the way it melted away his shyness and made him feel more outgoing, talkative, and energetic. When he used it, his friends said he was the life of the party, and girls seemed to like him more. So he started using it whenever he went to a party. Then he began snorting a few lines before school events, and then he did it every morning before he got to school. He rarely felt hungry anymore and lost about 15 pounds, leaving him rail thin.

When Cole was high, he talked a mile a minute and fidgeted in his seat in class. But when the effects wore off, he went back to his old, introverted self, felt depressed, and could barely muster the energy to get off the couch. He quit taking piano lessons, dropped out of the math club, and dumped his old friends in order to spend more time with his new drug buddies. When he couldn't get his hands on any cocaine, he couldn't stop thinking about it and lashed out at his parents and younger sister whenever they asked him if he was using drugs.

Let's take a closer look at the different symptoms of addiction.

BIOLOGICAL SYMPTOMS

Biological signs include changes to physical health and appearance and include, but are not limited to, the following:

- increase in cravings for the substance or behavior
- changes in eating or sleeping habits
- feeling sick or hung over
- forgetting what happened while under the influence
- using increasing amounts of a substance to get the same feeling
- inability to quit without feeling physically ill

PSYCHOLOGICAL SYMPTOMS

Addictions also result in many psychological issues:

- depression, irritability, or mood swings
- loss of interest in favorite activities
- minimizing the consequences of behavior
- annoyance or irritation when others question you
- feelings of guilt about behavior
- feeling anxious, depressed, or irritable when you are unable to engage in the behavior
- spending the day thinking about the behavior
- feeling powerless to change your behavior

SOCIAL SYMPTOMS

Harmful behaviors can cause many problems in your social life:

- negative changes in work or school performance
- withdrawal from family and friends
- neglecting responsibilities

- becoming friends with people who share your addiction
- spending more and more time engaging in the behavior
- avoiding situations where you can't engage in the behavior
- befriending the wrong people who are more likely to engage in harmful behavior

SPIRITUAL SYMPTOMS

In this context, *spiritual* doesn't mean "religious." It refers to your core values and morals, which are typically compromised in people with addictions and other troublesome behaviors. For example, before you became a slave to your habit, you probably never would have lied to your spouse, stolen money from a friend, or forgotten to pick up the kids from school. When you become entangled in problem behaviors, however, you start to do things you used to think were wrong. The following are a few symptoms of a broken moral compass:

- breaking rules at home, at school, or in the community
- cheating

- lying to family, friends, significant others, coworkers, and others
- stealing or selling cherished personal items to fuel your addiction
- hiding things
- breaking promises and making excuses
- using language only people with your addiction would understand

As you look at these lists of symptoms, be honest with yourself about the changes in your behavior and life. Take a pen and circle the symptoms that sound like you. The more symptoms you circle, the more likely there is a problem. Unless you recognize and admit that you have a problem, you will not be able to begin recovery.

Step 3: Make a Decision to Care For, Balance, and Repair Your Brain

To beat any addiction, it is critical to understand and optimize the brain. You must fall in love with it and work to balance and repair it. Eating right, exercising, avoiding anything that hurts your brain, and engaging in regular brain-healthy habits are critical to beating any addiction. However, at addiction-support groups, you're likely to see people smoking, drinking coffee, and offering one another unhealthy snacks.

I once helped a well-known addiction treatment center in Florida add brain SPECT imaging to their evaluation services. I was excited about the expansion of my work until I saw what they were feeding their clients for breakfast the morning of my first lecture: doughnuts, pastries, fruit juices, and sugary cereals. Sugar is another addictive substance. This habit must change. If you want to beat addictions, it is critical to get your brain right—and get the food right. In my book *The End of Mental Illness*, I include an entire chapter on simple brain-healthy rules that make food insanely simple. For more healthy habits to help you achieve weight loss, download our Brain Fit Life 5.0 app.

Step 4: Reach for Forgiveness for Yourself and Others

The easy answer for addictions is that people should just stop the difficult behavior. But addiction is much more complicated than most people think. Our brain-imaging work taught me that tough love works for people whose brains work right; but for people with troubled brains, tough love is like doing software programming on people with hardware problems, which is not very effective.

Critical to beating any addiction are self-love, self-care, and forgiveness of yourself and others. If you do not love yourself, you won't take proper care of your brain, and you will likely continue to hurt it. Forgiveness is the gift that keeps on giving; it is powerful medicine. Research shows a connection between forgiveness and reduced anxiety, depression, and psychiatric disorders. It is also associated with having fewer physical health symptoms and a lower mortality rate.

Step 5: Know Your Brain Type

All brains, even healthy ones, are not the same. When we first started to do brain-imaging work at Amen Clinics, we were looking for patterns associated with certain illnesses. We discovered they all have multiple patterns that require their own unique treatments. That made sense because, for example, there will never be just one pattern for depression because not all depressed people are the same. Some are withdrawn, others are angry, and still others are anxious or obsessive. Taking a one-size-fits-all approach invites failure and frustration.

The scans also helped us discover different brain types, which created nuances to patients' problems and treatments. This one idea led to a dramatic breakthrough in our effectiveness with patients, and it opened up a new world of understanding and hope for the tens of thousands of people who have come to see us and the millions of people who have read my books or seen my shows. Understanding these brain types is critical to getting the right help. I discuss the different brain types as well as practical strategies to treat the problems they can cause at length in *Your Brain Is Always Listening*, but for now, here is a quick overview.

BRAIN TYPE 1: BALANCED

People with this type tend to have healthy brains overall and be focused, flexible, positive, and relaxed. Their brains tend to be healthy, which makes them less likely to have addictions. However, it's important for these people to love and care for their brains with general brain-healthy strategies, such as regular exercise, a balanced diet, and ongoing new learning.

BRAIN TYPE 2: SPONTANEOUS

People with this brain type tend to be spontaneous, creative, out-of-the-box thinkers, restless, and easily distracted. They struggle to stay focused on something unless their interest in it is high. Our research team has published several studies showing that when people with this brain type try to concentrate, they actually have less activity in the prefrontal cortex, which causes them to need excitement or stimulation in order to focus (think of firefighters and race-car drivers). Smokers and heavy coffee drinkers also tend to fit this type of brain, as they use these substances to turn their brains "on."

BRAIN TYPE 3: PERSISTENT

Take-charge people who won't take no for an answer are likely to have this brain type. They tend to be tenacious and stubborn. In addition, they may worry, have trouble sleeping, be argumentative and oppositional, and hold grudges from the past. The persistent brain type often has increased activity in the anterior cingulate gyrus (ACG)—what I have described previously as the brain's gear shifter. It helps people go from thought to thought or move from action to action and is involved with being mentally flexible and going with the flow. When the ACG is overactive, usually due to low levels of serotonin, people can have problems shifting attention, which can make them persist—even when it may not be a good idea for them to do so.

BRAIN TYPE 4: SENSITIVE

Sensitive brain types generally show increased activity in the limbic or emotional centers of the brain, making these people sensitive, empathic, and deeply feeling but also subject to issues with their moods. They may also struggle with being more pessimistic and having negative thoughts.

BRAIN TYPE 5: CAUTIOUS

Cautious types often have heightened activity in the anxiety centers of the brain, such as the basal ganglia, insular cortex, or amygdala. The neurotransmitter gamma-aminobutyric acid (GABA) helps calm overfiring in the brain, and low levels of GABA frequently cause people with this brain type to struggle more with anxiety and subsequently be more cautious and reserved. However, on the flip side, they also tend to be more prepared.

Step 6: Control Your Cravings

All of us are vulnerable to cravings, but when you also have addictions, just seeing a glass pipe used for smoking cocaine, smelling cookies baking at the food court at the mall, or seeing an ad for a new video game will spark the emotional memory centers in your brain and trigger cravings to indulge in your old behavior. Even after decades of sobriety or steering clear of gambling, bulimia, video games, or porn, your brain is still vulnerable to cravings and those old patterns of behavior.

One of my patients, Molly, knew her risk. At 58, she had to have a surgical procedure. She was 32 years clean from a heroin addiction. When her doctor prescribed Vicodin—an opiate like heroin—for postsurgical pain relief, just taking one fired up the old, addicted pathway in her brain and ratcheted up cravings for the drug she had quit so many years before. Fortunately,

Molly had anticipated this could be a problem, and she had given the Vicodin to her husband and put him in charge of hiding them from her, counting them out each day, and dispensing them to her as directed on the bottle. After a couple of days, her pain was more bearable, and she switched to non-opiate, over-the-counter pain relievers, and the cravings subsided.

That's why it is critical to learn how to keep cravings at bay. The following nine strategies will help you get control of your cravings so you can avoid relapse.

1. Keep your blood sugar balanced. Low blood-sugar levels are associated with lower overall brain activity, including lower activity in the prefrontal cortex. Low brain activity here means more cravings, bad decisions, and relapse. Low blood-sugar levels can make you feel hungry, irritable, or anxious—all of which make you more likely to make poor choices. Low blood-sugar levels can also fuel anger and increase distractibility.

What causes low blood-sugar levels? Many everyday behaviors can cause dips in blood-sugar levels, including drinking alcohol, skipping meals, and consuming sugary snacks or beverages. High-sugar treats and drinks cause an initial spike in blood sugar but then a crash about 30 minutes later. Plus, the body uses glucose less efficiently as the day progresses, leading to more self-control failures in the evening and later at night. Keep your blood-sugar levels even throughout the day so you can reduce cravings and boost your self-control.

Eat a nutritious breakfast every day. Eating a nutrient-rich breakfast, including protein, helps your blood sugar get off to a good start and can keep it balanced for hours so you don't get hungry before lunchtime.

Have smaller meals throughout the day. This helps eliminate the blood-sugar roller coaster that can impact your emotions and increase your cravings.

Stay away from simple sugars and refined carbohydrates. This includes candy, sodas, cookies, crackers, white rice, white bread, and sweetened fruit juices. Foods that are high in sugar and fat work on the addiction centers of your brain. This is critical not only for people who are addicted to overeating, but also for people with other addictions. Bingeing on sugar has been found to alter brain chemistry and raise the risk for indulging in other drugs or alcohol. Sugar addiction is common in alcoholics and often develops when alcoholics try to quit drinking. Because the body metabolizes alcohol the same way as sugar, eating sugar can fuel alcohol cravings, and vice versa.

Avoid the dessert table. When I got this one idea through my own thick skull, I was finally able to lose the extra pounds I had been trying to shed for years. I love living without cravings. But for years, I fought the idea of giving up sweets, like Rocky Road ice cream or candy. I thought the key to losing weight was simply about calories in versus calories out. If I stayed within a certain calorie range, I'd be fine. The problem was that eating the sugar activated my cravings and made it very hard to stay away from foods that were bad for me. For most people, it takes about two weeks of completely avoiding sugar for your dessert cravings to go away.

2. Decrease the artificial sweeteners. If you really want to decrease your cravings, you also have to get rid of the artificial sweeteners in your diet.

We think of these sweeteners as free because they have no calories, but because they are up to 600 times sweeter than sugar, they may activate the appetite centers of the brain, making you crave even more food and more sugar. A group of Australian scientists found that alcohol floods the bloodstream faster when it is mixed with beverages containing artificial sweeteners rather than sugar.[2] Diet sodas are not the answer. The "natural" no-calorie sweetener I like best is stevia because it doesn't impact blood-sugar levels. However, I still recommend them only as an occasional treat.

3. Manage your stress. Another important way to decrease your cravings is to get on a daily stress-management program. Anything stressful can trigger certain hormones that activate your cravings, making you believe that you need the ice cream, cigarettes, or cocaine, or that you must take a virtual break, kick something to blow off steam, or call a friend to complain about your day. Prayer, meditation, and hypnosis are wonderful stress-management practices that can help boost your brain to control your cravings.

4. Outsmart sneaky addiction triggers. If you're an overeater, you can't go to the mall, airport, or ball game without seeing store after store and vendor after vendor advertising something that will fire up your cravings. For example, whenever I went to the movies, I used to immediately think about getting a big tub of popcorn with lots of butter along with licorice. But then I actually thought about the gobs of saturated fat, salt, and sugar that would be flooding my brain.

To control your cravings, you have to know the people, places, and things that fuel your cravings so you can plan ahead for vulnerable times. For example, I take a snack with me when I go to the movies now so I am not tempted by the popcorn and licorice.

5. Find out about hidden food allergies. Hidden food allergies and food sensitivities can trigger cravings and make you relapse. For example, did you know that wheat gluten and milk allergies can decrease blood flow to the brain and decrease your judgment? In addition, many of the symptoms associated with food allergies, such as headaches, sleep problems, lack of concentration, anger, aggression, and anxiety, can increase stress and cravings along with other harmful behaviors.

Food allergies are closely linked to alcoholism. Corn, wheat, rye, and barley are common sources of food allergies and happen to be ingredients used to make alcohol like vodka, whiskey, beer, gin, and bourbon. The foods that you are allergic to are often the ones you crave the most, so if you are allergic to an ingredient in alcohol, you may crave alcohol.

6. *Train willpower.* Willpower is like a muscle. You have to use it or lose it. Most of us learn to develop self-control as children. When our parents say no to us when we ask if we can do something that isn't good for us—have a plate of cookies before dinner, ride on the back of a neighbor's motorcycle without a helmet, or grab the tail of a strange dog—we learn to say no to ourselves. But maybe your parents weren't around much because they were workaholics and you had free rein to do whatever you wanted so you never learned self-control. Or perhaps your parents had addictions, and you learned to give in to your desires by watching their

behavior. Maybe your addiction has robbed you of your ability to say no. Or perhaps your bad habits have trained your brain to give in to your cravings.

No matter what the reason is for your lack of self-restraint, pump up your willpower by practicing it. Say no over and over to the things that are not good for you. The more you do this, the easier it will be. Once you've said no, immediately do something else to move your focus off your craving. Redirect your attention.

7. Get moving. Scientific research on exercise and addiction has found that physical activity can cut cravings and reduce the risk for relapse. Whether you crave cigarettes, alcohol, sugary snacks, drugs, or gambling, exercise can help. One study of moderately heavy smokers who had abstained from smoking for 15 hours showed that even when faced with smoking-related images that would typically trigger cravings, the smokers had less desire to light up after exercising.[3]

8. Get adequate sleep. Have you ever noticed that after a night with almost no sleep, you wake up ravenously hungry and want to eat anything and everything in sight? That is because lack of sleep increases food cravings and cravings for other addictive behaviors. When you sleep well, your brain cleans itself and reinforces memory and learning in preparation for the next day, leading to better decision-making.

9. Take natural supplements for craving control. N-acetyl-cysteine, alpha-lipoic acid, and chromium are three natural supplements that can help take the edge off cravings. Here's how they work.

N-acetyl-cysteine (NAC): NAC is an amino acid that is needed to produce glutathione, a powerful antioxidant. NAC binds to and removes dangerous toxic elements within the cells. NAC has been studied as a treatment for drug addiction because it functions to restore levels of the excitatory neurotransmitter glutamate in the reward center of the brain.[4] A growing body of research has found that NAC can reduce cravings for cocaine, heroin, and cigarettes and decrease the risk for relapse. It also reduces compulsive behavior in pathological gamblers and may be helpful in reducing food cravings. In one study, researchers conducted a double-blind placebo-controlled clinical trial on NAC and its effects on 27 pathological gamblers. After the eight-week trial, 83 percent of those taking NAC compared to only 29 percent of placebo takers experienced at least a 30 percent reduction in addictive behavior.[5] The typical adult dose is 600–1,200 mg twice a day to curb cravings.

Alpha-lipoic acid: Made naturally in the body, alpha-lipoic acid may protect against cell damage in a variety of conditions. Strong evidence indicates that alpha-lipoic acid supports stable blood-sugar levels. Studies have shown that it improves insulin sensitivity and may be effective in treating type 2 diabetes.[6] The typical recommended adult dose is 100 mg twice a day.

Chromium: Chromium picolinate is a nutritional supplement used to aid the body in the regulation of insulin, which enhances metabolism of glucose and fat. A strong link exists between depression, decreased insulin sensitivity, and diabetes. Supplementation with chromium picolinate effectively modulates carbohydrate cravings and appetite, which is beneficial to managing both diabetes and depression. The typical recommended adult dosage is 200–600 mcg a day.

HALT is a common acronym in addiction recovery circles for relapse prevention. Do not let yourself get too hungry (low blood sugar is associated with low blood flow to the prefrontal cortex and more bad decisions), angry (anger lowers PFC function), lonely (being disconnected from others increases bad decisions), or tired (lack of sleep is associated with low PFC function). All of these factors impair decision-making skill and your ability to control cravings.

Step 7: Drip Dopamine; Stop Dumping It to Keep Your Pleasure Centers Healthy.

Dopamine is a feel-good chemical that our addictions crave. Whenever we do something enjoyable, it's like pressing a button in the brain to release a little bit of dopamine to make us feel pleasure. If we push these pleasure buttons too often or too strongly, we reduce dopamine's effectiveness and wear out our pleasure centers. Eventually, it takes more and more excitement and stimulation to feel anything at all. Cocaine, methamphetamines, alcohol, and nicotine all cause dopamine surges that make these substances highly desirable—sometimes even more desirable than things like food, water, and sex. When people take drugs, the amount of dopamine released can be two to ten times more than what their brain produces for natural rewards.

Drugs and alcohol aren't the only substances that can hijack your brain. Playing video games, gambling, and looking at internet pornography can produce the same effect. So can certain foods. In *The End of Overeating*, former FDA commissioner Dr. David Kessler writes that the high-fat, high-sugar combinations found in many mouth-watering snacks light up the brain's dopamine pathway similar to the way drugs and alcohol do. He suggests that some people can actually get hooked on chocolate chip cookies the way other people get addicted to cocaine.[7]

Parkinson's disease teaches us a lot about dopamine because cells in an area of the brain called the substantia nigra, which produce dopamine, start to die, causing people to lose control over their muscle movements (shaking, stiffness, difficulty walking, balance). Low dopamine levels are also associated with depression, lack of motivation, low energy, and trouble focusing. One of my college professors, a very proper, loving man, developed a Parkinson's-like syndrome. When I treated him decades later, he loved Dr. Phil and Jerry Springer, which horrified his family. The conflict-driven television shows likely increased his dopamine levels, making him feel more alive.

The concept is simple. When we eat a bowl of fresh berries or hold our spouse's hand, our brains release small amounts of dopamine, which make us feel good. I call that dripping dopamine. It won't drain the dopamine stores in our brain. When we do a line of cocaine, watch porn, or eat caramel fudge brownies, our brains pump out lots of dopamine, which makes us feel great. That dumps dopamine, which can drain our dopamine stores and increases the relative importance or salience of cocaine, porn, and caramel fudge brownies in our minds. Soon we no longer get much pleasure from eating berries or holding our spouse's hand and begin craving cocaine, porn, or caramel fudge brownies instead. Here is an illustration of the addiction cycle.

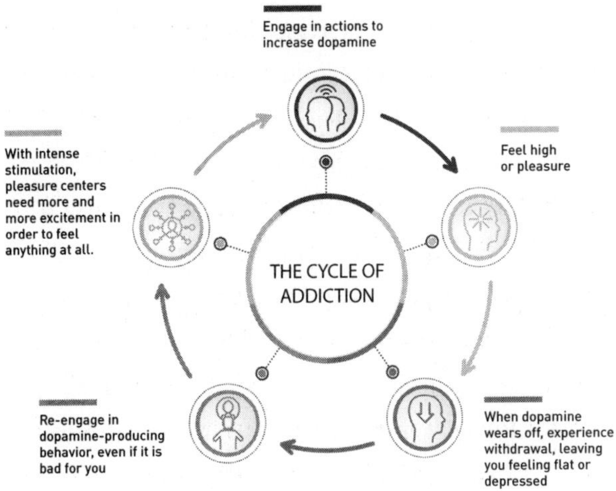

Some simple actions can help you protect your pleasure centers and keep them healthy:

- Limit low-value dopamine activities, such as caffeine, nicotine, excessive television, video games, undisciplined digital behavior, and scary movies.
- Limit activities that dump dopamine, including skydiving, motorcycle racing, heli-skiing, running with bulls, drug and alcohol use, porn, and sugar.

- Engage in high-value dopamine activities that drip dopamine, such as sunlight (vitamin D), exercise, meditation, yoga, massage therapy, pleasurable music, hugs and hand-holding, and regular physical exercise, especially something you love that does not endanger your brain, such as dancing, swimming, or tennis.
- Make time to laugh—humor enhances the pleasure centers without wearing them out.
- Connect meaningful activities and pleasure, such as volunteering for activities you love. One example: I love table tennis and enjoy keeping score for others during tournaments.
- Start every day by thinking of three things for which you are grateful (a small dopamine drip) and one person you appreciate (another small dopamine drip), then reach out to tell that person you appreciate them with a text or email. You are building a bridge of gratitude, and if they respond, it is yet another, maybe bigger, dopamine drip.

- Seek pleasure in the little things in your life, such as a walk with a friend, holding hands with your spouse, a great meal, or a meaningful church service.
- Eat foods that contain dopamine-boosting properties, such as chicken, turkey, seafood, almonds, pumpkin and sesame seeds, turmeric, oregano, vegetables (for folate and magnesium), olive oil, and green tea (careful not to consume too much caffeinated tea).
- Consider supplements to support dopamine, such as omega-3 fatty acids, SAMe, L-tyrosine, magnesium, bacopa, and green tea extract.

Step 8: Eliminate the Negative Influences That Make You Vulnerable

Cultivating bad habits—and good ones—is a team sport. You become like the people you spend time with. Negative influences are people who encourage or are complicit with your negative behaviors.

Take my patient Riz, for example. He had no problem sticking with his new eating regimen until he went to dinner parties with friends and family. Then his loved ones would offer him all kinds of foods and alcoholic drinks that he used to love but that didn't fit into his new brain-healthy lifestyle. Riz's friends and family would try to pressure and coax him into eating or drinking things he had given up. "What's wrong with you?" they would ask. "You're not obese. Why aren't you having any kebab? Why aren't you eating any rice? You've always loved kebab and rice." They made Riz feel like he was being rude if he didn't give in and take a helping . . . or two.

I know that feeling very well. When I became a grandfather for the first time, I couldn't wait to visit my new grandson, Elias. When I went to my daughter's home, a friend of mine was also visiting. She asked me if I wanted something to eat, and I said no, I wasn't hungry. A few minutes later, she asked me again, and I told her no again. I thought that would be the end of that discussion, but she continued to ask me an additional five times if I wanted something to eat!

You will face many types of negative influences who will attempt to derail your health efforts. Do not let other people make you fat, stupid, and unhappy!

If you want to change your behavior, you need to stop seeing your negative influences or somehow turn them into friends. Consider talking to your negative influences. Explain what they can start doing to help you, what they can stop doing, and what they can continue doing. Some don't even realize that they are influencing you to make poor choices and will want to help once they understand your goals to kick addiction. If they are not interested or willing to help you, stop spending time around them if possible.

Here are some tips on how to deal with negative influences:

- If you are going to a dinner with friends or family, call ahead to inform the host that you are on a special brain-healthy diet and won't be drinking alcohol or eating certain foods. You only have to do this once or twice before your friends start to ask you what they could serve that is brain-healthy.
- When going to parties, consider eating something ahead of time so you won't

be hungry or tempted by alcohol at the event.

- Be up front with negative influences. Explain that you are trying to eat a more balanced diet or stay away from alcohol and drugs, and that when they offer you cake, chips, pizza, alcohol, or marijuana, it makes it more difficult for you.
- Instead of going out to lunch or happy hour with friends, choose activities that aren't centered around food or alcohol, such as going for a walk.
- When people offer seconds (food or drink), tell them you are finished. If they insist, explain that you are watching your health. If they continue to push you, gently ask them why they don't want you to be healthy.
- Avoid visiting with coworkers who have a bowl of candy on their desk.
- Eat very slowly so when the host starts asking guests if they want seconds, you can say you are still working on your first helping. By the time you have finished,

the second round of eating could be over, and you won't have to be subjected to the offer for more.

- Commit to taking control of your own body and don't let other people steal your mind.
- Tell restaurant servers "no bread" or "no alcohol" when seated.
- Inform parents and in-laws ahead of time that you won't be partaking in certain foods or drink at family gatherings.
- Bring a sack lunch instead of eating out or eating at the cafeteria.
- If alcohol is a problem, don't meet friends at a bar.
- Avoid associating with acquaintances who engage in the addictive behaviors you are trying to quit.
- Unsubscribe from any online gambling or sports-betting sites if that's a problem for you.
- Remove yourself from any group chats or texts with fellow gamers if you are trying to limit your game playing.

Friends, mentors, or coaches are people who support your positive behaviors. Ask for their help. In my work with The Daniel Plan, a program I created with Pastor Rick Warren and Dr. Mark Hyman to help people get healthy through thousands of religious organizations, we found that adding friends improves your chances for success up to 40 percent, and this is especially true for drug addictions, weight loss, and fitness.

Identify your five most powerful friends who will support your good behaviors and commit to spending more time with them.

Step 9: Deal with Past Trauma and Eliminate Negative Self-Talk

To get and stay free of addiction, you have to deal with the past trauma that likely led to your addiction and start eliminating negative self-talk.

For example, one of my patients, Corinne, 52, had smoked since she was a teenager. By the time she came to see me, she had been smoking for almost 40 years, and she had the wrinkled skin and breathing problems to prove it. Her loved ones desperately wanted her to stop smoking.

Corinne wanted to quit but didn't believe she could do it. "I can't stop," she told me in one of our first sessions.

Corinne had started smoking after her mother, who also smoked, abandoned her to run off with a new boyfriend, leaving Corinne with an aunt to raise her. As a teen, Corinne had felt so much anxiety that her aunt would also abandon her that she used smoking to soothe herself.

To quit smoking, Corinne would have to deal with the anxiety that kept her addicted to cigarettes. We worked together on her anxiety, and we tackled her negative self-talk using a five-question method I adapted from Byron Katie's book *Loving What Is*:[8]

1. Is it true?
2. Is it absolutely true with 100 percent certainty?
3. How do I feel when I believe this thought?
4. How would I feel if I couldn't have this thought?
5. Turn the thought around to its exact opposite, and then ask if the opposite

of the thought is true or even truer than the original thought. Then use this turnaround as a meditation.

Here's how it played out (with my questions in italics):

"I can't stop smoking."

1. *Is it true?* "Yes."

2. *Can you absolutely know it's true?* Initially, she said yes; she knew she couldn't do it. Then she thought about it and said, "Of course, I can't know for sure, especially if I got the right help."

3. *How do you feel when you have the thought?* "I feel powerless, sad, weak-willed, stupid, out of control, like a bad influence on my children."

4. *Who would you be without the thought?* "I would be hopeful, optimistic, more likely to give it my best effort."

5. *What is the opposite thought? Is it truer than the original thought?* "I can stop smoking." She

> thought about this for a while and said that if she got help and really tried, it could be true. Then she felt a sense of control and committed to a program.

Corinne eventually did stop smoking and felt better than ever.

Step 10: Get Help from Those Who Have Beaten Their Own Addictions

Success leaves clues. Addiction mentors and support groups are often critical pieces to the healing process. The people you meet at support groups have walked your path and may have strategies that can help you. Other people who have struggled with your issue can help you feel less lonely and give you an outlet to express your thoughts. Often just hearing what you are thinking out loud, with the input of others, can help eliminate a lot of your negative self-talk. In fact, research shows that support groups can decrease anxiety and depression. They can help you stay motivated to stick to a new way of living. They can give you hope. They are also an affordable and often free way of getting help.

Choose your helpers wisely. As we've seen, you become like the people you spend time with. Choose people who represent how you want to live, not those who increase your risk of relapse.

Here are some tips for choosing mentors or support groups:

1. Pick people who've been successful at beating addictions like yours. The longer they've kept the addictions at bay, the better.
2. Pick people who will tell you the truth with kindness. Sugarcoating is not helpful (and you know what I think of sugar), but neither is being condescending or mean.
3. Don't be afraid of those who are younger than you.
4. Choose people who will challenge you.
5. Choose people with similar values.
6. Choose people with two ears and one mouth, who take time to listen.
7. Choose people who you are not afraid to call or text.

8. Once you choose someone, be open to their input but also evaluate it. Don't be so open-minded your brain falls out of your skull.
9. Meet mentors at in-person or online support groups, through mutual friends, church, or other organizations. Be kind to everyone you meet because you never know when a mentor will appear.
10. Take an interest in those you respect. Most people who ask for mentoring are only interested in themselves. The best way to put off a mentor is to do it in a self-centered way. Finding a great mentor begins when you take an interest in someone you respect. Then consider how you can add value to their lives. That way you don't have to ask them to mentor you, but they volunteer.

Bottom line, one of the fastest ways to get healthy is to find the healthiest person you can stand and spend as much time around them as possible.

Step 11: List the People Your Addiction(s) Have Hurt, Share It with a Mentor or Sponsor, and Make Amends if You Can

This is a combination of AA steps that is essential to improve your relationships and to have a better sense of yourself—let's do this step with a better-balanced brain. None of us exists in a vacuum. Admitting your wrongs to others, asking for forgiveness, and making amends if you're able makes you less likely to continue the behavior that is hurtful to others.

Step 12: Carry the Message of Brain Health to Others and Continue to Practice These 12 Steps

This last step is similar to the Twelfth Step of AA and other anonymous programs. If you want to keep your sobriety, you need to share the principles with others. It completely works for brain health too. Your brain is always listening to what you do, but it is also listening to the actions of others. Make sure you are sharing brain health, not illness, with those you love.

Get it, give it away, and keep it forever. This is a mantra I learned after creating The Daniel Plan with my friends Pastor Rick Warren and

Dr. Mark Hyman, a program to get the world healthy through churches and religious organizations. If you want to keep your health, you have to learn how to do it and then give it away to others. For it is in the act of giving that you create your own support group, making it more likely you will stay on the program.

You Can Do It!

Whether you are simply trying to kick a bad habit or are taking the first steps towards tackling a lifelong addiction, I hope the strategies I have shared in this book will help you achieve your goals. In fact, I'm confident they will—I've seen it.

Brain health has been my passion for 40 years. Looking at the brain changed the way I practiced medicine and psychiatry, as well as the way I live my life. Now, over 250,000 brain scans later, it's become even more clear that the problems we treat aren't *mental health* issues; they're *brain health* issues that steal your mind.

Enhancing biological brain health is a foundational aspect of how we help our patients get better at Amen Clinics, but it is only one piece of the wellness puzzle. Conquering bad habits is another piece of that puzzle, and learning how to keep your undesirable behaviors in check is key to staying on the right path.

Temptations will continue to assault you every day. It's unavoidable. Some days they'll be whispering inside your head. Other days, when stress and anxiety are through the roof, they'll be screaming incessantly. Whether you listen to them depends on the health of your brain and the strength of your prefrontal cortex. But if you take good care of your brain, adhere to your One Page Miracle, and follow the steps and strategies outlined in this book, you'll be able to drown out the lies, the negative self-talk, and the noise; make healthier decisions; enhance your relationships; and conquer your bad habits once and for all.

APPENDIX 1

STRATEGIES FOR BETTER BRAIN HEALTH

CONQUERING BAD HABITS starts with the physical functioning of your brain and keeping it in optimal condition. Years ago, I created the mnemonic BRIGHT MINDS to help people remember these simple yet effective strategies.

Improve **B**lood Flow
Slow **R**etirement and Aging
Reduce **I**nflammation
Know **G**enetics
Avoid **H**ead Trauma
Reduce Exposure to **T**oxins

Treat Mental Health Issues
Optimize Immunity and Prevent Infections
Balance Your Neurohormones
Prevent Diabesity
Get Good Sleep

I have written extensively about these strategies in *Memory Rescue*, *The End of Mental Illness*, and *You, Happier*, so I will only summarize the main points here.

Blood Flow

Blood brings nourishment to every cell in your body and takes away waste products, so anything that damages blood vessels also damages your brain and starves it of the nutrients it needs. Low blood flow is associated with depression, but when you *improve* blood flow to the brain, it can make you happier. How do you improve blood flow?

- Hydrate. Your brain is 80 percent water.
- Limit caffeine and nicotine. Both constrict blood flow to the brain.

- Exercise, even if it's just a brisk 15-minute walk every day.
- Take ginkgo biloba supplements.
- Watch a comedy. Laughing while viewing funny movies increases vascular function.[1]

Retirement and Aging

Brain imaging work reveals that your brain typically becomes less and less active with age. To decrease the risks from retirement and aging, research shows that these strategies can help:

- Enrolling in lifelong learning and memory training programs.
- Being socially connected and volunteering.
- Meditating.
- Taking a daily multivitamin.
- Eating foods that contain vitamin C, such as strawberries and red bell peppers.

Inflammation

You may know that too much inflammation is associated with cancer and arthritis, but did you know that it is also linked to depression? You can control a number of important and surprising causes of chronic inflammation:

- Eliminate sugar and processed foods. Get your food right, and your mind will follow.
- Floss! Poor oral health has been linked to depression and anxiety.[2] You must floss and take care of your teeth.
- Take probiotics. Maintaining good gut health is critical to lowering inflammation.
- Think positively! Being able to point to frequent moments of positivity throughout the day is associated with lower levels of inflammation.[3]

Genetics

A 2015 study in *Behavior Genetics* found that genetics accounted for about one third of a person's life satisfaction.[4]

- If you think you're at genetic risk for brain issues, early screening is essential.

- Test your genes with online genetic testing services to know your vulnerabilities and meet with a medical professional to help you interpret the results.
- Take responsibility for your happiness. If 40 percent of your sense of well-being lies in genetics, that means 60 percent is in your hands.

Head Trauma

Head injuries, even mild ones that occurred decades ago, are a major cause of depression. If you've had a head injury, the good news is that many things can help it heal, even years later. Practicing the BRIGHT MINDS strategies has been shown to bring about significant improvement in blood flow, mood, memory, attention, and sleep. And when you feel better, have better recall, and sleep better, you are more likely to be happier.

Toxins

Toxins are some of the most common causes of depression, anxiety, brain fog, and irritability.

Many things are toxic to your brain, such as drugs, alcohol, smoking, mold exposure, carbon monoxide, and heavy metals like mercury and lead.

To decrease your toxic risk, limit your exposure whenever you can; buy organic foods to decrease pesticide consumption; avoid ingredients like phthalates, parabens, and aluminum; drink more water; eat plenty of fiber; and get plenty of exercise (sweat the bad stuff out).

Mental Health Issues

Untreated mental health issues, such as depression, anxiety, OCD, ADD/ADHD, addictions, and chronic stress can hurt the brain and make you unhappy. If you struggle with any of these issues, it's critical to get them treated by a professional.

Also, if you're struggling with anxiety, the most common mental health disorder, try the following:

- Check for low blood sugar, anemia, and hyperthyroidism, as these can cause anxiety.

- Meditation and slow, deep belly breathing can immediately increase a sense of calmness.
- Calming exercises such as yoga can help.
- Start with nutritional supplements like L-theanine, GABA, and magnesium before resorting to antianxiety medications that are hard to stop.

Immunity and Infections

When your immune system is weak, you're more likely to get infections. When it's overactive, you increase your risk for depression, anxiety, and even psychosis, and having any kind of illness saps the joy out of your life. Some of the best ways to strengthen your immunity include:

- Optimizing your vitamin D level.
- Taking probiotics, because gut health is critical to your immunity.
- Trying an elimination diet for a month to see if food allergies may be damaging your immune system (eliminate gluten, dairy, corn, soy, sugar and artificial sweeteners, dyes, and preservatives).

Neurohormone Issues

Without healthy hormones, you feel temperamental, tired, and foggy. To keep your hormones healthy:

- Test them every year after the age of 40.
- Avoid animal proteins that were raised with hormones or antibiotics.
- Add fiber to decrease unhealthy estrogens.
- Lift weights and limit sugar to boost testosterone.
- Use hormone replacement when needed.

Diabesity

Excessive fat disrupts your hormones, stores toxins, and produces chemicals that increase inflammation. When obesity is combined with diabetes, the risk is worse. High blood sugar levels damage your blood vessels. Research shows that obesity increases the odds of depression,[5] and some studies indicate that the risk of depression doubles for those with diabetes.[6] To get diabesity under control, you have to eat healthy foods and exercise regularly.

Sleep

When you sleep, your brain cleans or washes itself. If sleep is disrupted, trash builds up in your brain. If you want to improve your brain and feel better tomorrow, improve your sleep tonight. To sleep better:

- Make your room cooler, darker, and quieter.
- Turn off your gadgets so they don't disturb you.
- Listen to music with a slow, relaxing rhythm.
- If bad thoughts keep you awake, journal to get them out of your head.

To live a happy, healthier life, you must take good care of your brain. Use the BRIGHT MINDS approach to get and keep your brain healthy so you can start conquering your bad habits once and for all!

APPENDIX 2

50 TINY HABITS THAT CAN LEAD TO BIG CHANGES

OUR BRAINS ARE WIRED to keep doing what we've always done—and often what we've done has not been very healthy, which is how we end up stuck in behavioral ruts of our own making. The good news is, we can change those negative ruts into superhighways of success. And it starts by committing to making tiny changes every day.

Each of these habits takes just a few minutes. They are anchored to something you do (or think or feel) so that they are more likely to become automatic. They are all easy changes that will boost your sense of accomplishment and competence and, over time, evolve into bigger changes.

Remember, small daily improvements are the key to spectacular long-term results.

1. After I answer the phone, I will stand up and walk while I talk.
2. After I start to argue, I will ask myself, *Is my behavior getting me what I want?*
3. When I get out of bed in the morning, I will open the curtains/shades to let the sunshine in.
4. When I feel anxious, I will eat a complex carbohydrate, such as a sweet potato, to boost serotonin.
5. When I relapse or make a mistake with my health, I will ask myself, *What can I learn from my mistake?*
6. When I am tempted to eat unhealthy foods, I will eat the healthy ones on my plate first.
7. When I am dealing with someone who is stuck on a negative thought or arguing,

I will ask them to go for a walk with me and will not bring up any charged topic for at least 10 minutes.

8. When I want to go out to eat, I will ask the healthiest person I know to go with me.
9. When I feel thoughts going over and over in my head, I will write them down, which helps to get rid of them.
10. After I've had a fight with a loved one, I will take responsibility for my part and apologize.
11. When someone acts negatively toward me, I will ask myself, *Did I do anything to cause it? What is going on with this person?*
12. When I am in a conversation with someone, before responding with my input, I will reflect back what I heard them saying.
13. When I am challenged or bullied, I will state the case for what I believe, calmly and clearly.

14. When I set aside time to be with my child, I will spend 20 minutes doing whatever they want to do, with no agenda.
15. When I have a negative thought about my spouse, such as *They never listen to me*, I will write it down and ask myself, *Is that true?* If it is not, I will quash the thought.
16. When a friend does something annoying, I will turn my attention to the things I like about them rather than dwelling on the annoyance.
17. When someone is mean or hurtful to me, I will try to create grace in my heart to forgive them.
18. When I need to get work done, I will put my smartphone on "Do not disturb" as a discipline to be more focused and to stop the constant pings or drips of dopamine it tries to addict me to.
19. When I am on the train or bus to work, I will read my One Page Miracle and

ask myself, *Will my behavior today get me what I want?*

20. When I start getting upset about something happening in my day, I'll ask myself, *Does this have eternal value?*
21. When it is sunny outdoors, I will take a walk to soak up the sunshine and boost my vitamin D level.
22. When I start the coffee or tea in the morning, I'll think of three things for which I'm grateful.
23. Once a week, I will watch a comedy to boost my dopamine level. (*Whose Line Is It Anyway?* is a great show to start with.)
24. Before I go to bed, I will write down one purposeful thing I did that day.
25. When I am tempted by french fries, sugary treats, or soda, I will resist and say to myself, *I love only foods that love me back.*
26. Before I leave the house, I will put a full water bottle inside my purse or computer bag.

27. When I prepare my food shopping list, I will include fish and vegetables.
28. When I finish dinner, I will note the time and make plans to eat my next meal at least 12 hours later to give my brain time for waste removal.
29. When I pick up a new item at the grocery store, I will read the food label.
30. When I'm in a low mood, I will eat a piece of low-sugar or sugar-free dark chocolate to boost my serotonin level.
31. When I eat a food I love that loves me back, I will note it down in my "favorite healthy foods" list.
32. When the waiter comes for my order at a restaurant, I will say, "Please don't bring bread to the table." Making that one decision will help me make healthier choices throughout the meal.
33. When I go food shopping, I will look for organic fruits and vegetables first.
34. When I approach any meal, I will ask myself if I am getting the nutrients I

need to serve my health rather than steal from my health.

35. When I bring food to work, school, or an event, I will ask myself if it serves the health of those who will eat it or if it steals from their health.
36. When I shower in the morning, I will ask myself if I am doing what I can to be a healthy role model for my family.
37. Whenever I am around my friends, I will ask myself if I am modeling behavior that helps their health or makes it worse.
38. When I hold my spouse's hand, I will gently squeeze it and remember that if our habits are healthy, our love life will be better and last longer throughout our lives.
39. When I watch the news, I will be on the lookout for ways to make a meaningful contribution to the health of my community.
40. When I am tempted by something that is bad for my brain (like candy or

cigarettes), I will hum to myself for a few minutes until the temptation passes.

41. After I open my refrigerator, I will throw out one food that is bad for my brain.
42. When someone at work, church, or home asks me to take on a new task, I will say, "I have to think about it."
43. When I go to a party, I will ask for a wine spritzer and top it up with club soda so I'm sure I don't drink too much.
44. When I slip up on my goals, I will note it down in my journal.
45. When my child asks if they can play a contact sport like football or soccer, I will say, "No, I want to protect your brain from harm."
46. When I feel out of sorts, I will take 10 deep breaths and focus on my goals.
47. When I eat breakfast, I will take a supplement to improve my brain.
48. When someone is being difficult with me, I will try not to overreact, knowing

the other person may have issues I am unaware of.

49. When my feet hit the floor first thing in the morning, I will say to myself, *Today is going to be a great day.*
50. Whenever I come to a decision point in my day, I will ask myself, *Is the decision I'm about to make good for my brain or bad for it?*

NOTES

CHAPTER 1: YOUR BRAIN—A VERY BRIEF PRIMER

1. Robin L. Aupperle and P. Paulus Martin, "Neural Systems Underlying Approach and Avoidance in Anxiety Disorders," *Dialogues in Clinical Neuroscience* 12, no. 4 (2010): 517–531, https://doi.org/10.31887/DCNS.2010.12.4/raupperle.
2. Hui Lei et al., "Altered Spontaneous Brain Activity in Obsessive-Compulsive Personality Disorder," *Comprehensive Psychiatry* 96 (January 2020): 152144, https://doi.org/10.1016/j.comppsych.2019.152144.
3. Anders Wåhlin and Lars Nyberg, "At the Heart of Cognitive Functioning in Aging," *Trends in Cognitive Sciences* 23, no. 9 (September 2019): 717–720, https://doi.org/10.1016/j.tics.2019.06.004.
4. Cyrus A. Raji et al., "Clinical Utility of SPECT Neuroimaging in the Diagnosis and Treatment of Traumatic Brain Injury: A Systematic Review," *PLOS ONE* 9, no. 3 (2014): e91088, https://doi.org/10.1371/journal.pone.0091088.

5. "What Are Sleep Deprivation and Deficiency?," National Heart, Lung, and Bood Institute, NIH, last updated March 24, 2022, https://www.nhlbi.nih.gov/health/sleep-deprivation.

CHAPTER 2: ON YOUR MARK, LET'S SET . . . GOALS!

1. I've written about the One Page Miracle in many of my books, starting with *Change Your Brain, Change Your Life* (Times Books, 1998), chap. 8.

CHAPTER 3: 5 SIMPLE STEPS TO CONQUERING YOUR BAD HABITS

1. James Clear, *Atomic Habits* (Avery, 2018).

CHAPTER 4: HOW TO CONQUER 10 COMMON BAD HABITS

1. Bella M. DePaulo et al., "Lying in Everyday Life," *Journal of Personality and Social Psychology* 70, no. 5 (June 1996): 979–995, https://doi.org/10.1037/0022-3514.70.5.979.
2. Andrea Gurmankin Levy et al., "Prevalence of and Factors Associated with Patient Nondisclosure of Medically Relevant Information to Clinicians," *JAMA Network Open* 1, no. 7 (November 2, 2018): e185293, https://doi.org/10.1001/jamanetworkopen.2018.5293.
3. "Landmark Report: U.S. Teens Use an Average of Nine Hours of Media per Day, Tweens Use Six Hours: New 'Media Use Census' from Common Sense Details Media Habits and Preferences of American 8- to 18-Year-Olds," Common Sense Media, November 3, 2015, https://www.commonsensemedia.org/about-us/news/press-releases/landmark-report-us-teens-use-an-average-of-nine-hours-of-media-per-day.
4. James B. Weaver III et al., "Health-Risk Correlates of Video-Game Playing among Adults," *American Journal*

of Preventive Medicine 37, no. 4 (October 2009): 299–305, https://doi.org/10.1016/j.amepre.2009.06.014.

5. Ian Bogost, "The Cigarette of This Century," *Atlantic*, June 6, 2012, https://www.theatlantic.com/technology/archive/2012/06/the-cigarette-of-this-century/258092/.
6. Kevin McSpadden, "You Now Have a Shorter Attention Span than a Goldfish," *Time*, May 14, 2015, https://time.com/3858309/attention-spans-goldfish/.
7. McSpadden, "You Now Have a Shorter Attention."
8. Heike Bruch and Sumantra Ghoshal, "Beware the Busy Manager," *Harvard Business Review*, February 2002, https://hbr.org/2002/02/beware-the-busy-manager.
9. Yaser Ghanam, "Why Agile Methods Work," InfoQ, December 12, 2012, https://www.infoq.com/articles/why-agile-methods-work/.
10. National Center for Health Statistics, "Obesity and Overweight," Centers for Disease Control and Prevention, October 25, 2024, http://www.cdc.gov/nchs/fastats/obesity-overweight.htm.
11. Tyler Muse, "How 'Betcha Can't Eat Just One' Addicted Us to Junk Food," History Oasis, accessed January 31, 2025, https://www.historyoasis.com/post/betcha-cant-eat-just-one.
12. Ronald Jandacek et al., "Interactions of Body Weight Loss with Lipophilic Toxin Storage: Commentary," *Journal of Nutrition* 154, no. 3 (March 2024): 801–803, https://doi.org/10.1016/j.tjnut.2024.01.018; "Obesity and Hormones," Better Health Channel, accessed December 31, 2024, https://www.betterhealth.vic.gov.au/health/healthyliving/obesity-and-hormones#bhc-content.
13. Danielle Dresden, "Effects of Diabetes on the Body and Organs," Medical News Today, updated May 4,

2023, https://www.medicalnewstoday.com/articles/317483#summary.

14. Craig M. Hales et al., "Prevalence of Obesity Among Adults and Youth: United States 2015–2016," NCHS Data Brief, no. 288, October 2017, https://www.cdc.gov/nchs/data/databriefs/db288.pdf.
15. Gregory E. Simon et al., "Association between Obesity and Psychiatric Disorders in the US Adult Population," *Archives of General Psychiatry* 63, no. 7 (July 2006): 824–830, https://doi.org/10.1001/archpsyc.63.7.824; Nancy M. Petry et al., "Overweight and Obesity Are Associated with Psychiatric Disorders: Results from the National Epidemiologic Survey on Alcohol and Related Conditions," *Psychosomatic Medicine* 70, no. 3 (April 2008): 288–297, https://doi.org/10.1097/PSY.0b013e3181651651.
16. H. C. Michelle Byrd et al., "Attention-Deficit/Hyperactivity Disorder and Obesity in US Males and Females, Age 8–15 Years: National Health and Nutrition Examination Survey 2001–2004," *Pediatric Obesity* 8, no. 6 (December 2013): 445–453, https://doi.org/10.1111/j.2047-6310.2012.00124.x.
17. Michael Hinck, "How Obesity Can Affect Your Teen's Self Esteem," *Health Beat*, Jamaica Hospital Medical Center, September 26, 2014, https://jamaicahospital.org/newsletter/how-obesity-can-affect-your-teens-self-esteem/.
18. Zhang Xue-Yan et al., "Obese Chinese Primary-School Students and Low Self-Esteem: A Cross-Sectional Study," *Iranian Journal of Pediatrics* 26, no. 4 (August 2016): e3777, https://doi.org/10.5812/ijp.3777.
19. Kenneth M. Carpenter et al., "Relationships between Obesity and DSM-IV Major Depressive Disorder,

Suicide Ideation, and Suicide Attempts: Results from a General Population Study," *American Journal of Public Health* 90, no. 2 (2000): 251–257, https://doi.org/10.2105/ajph.90.2.251.

20. Cyrus A. Raji et al., "Brain Structure and Obesity," *Human Brain Mapping* 31, no. 3 (March 2010): 353–364, https://doi.org/10.1002/hbm.20870; Kristen C. Willeumier et al., "Elevated BMI Is Associated with Decreased Blood Flow in the Prefrontal Cortex Using SPECT Imaging in Healthy Adults," *Obesity* 19, no. 5 (May 2011): 1095–1097, https://doi.org/10.1038/oby.2011.16; Mark Hamer and G. David Batty, "Association of Body Mass Index and Waist-to-Hip Ratio with Brain Structure," *Neurology* 92, no. 6 (February 2019): e594–600, https://doi.org/10.1212/WNL.0000000000006879.
21. Alan R. Schwartz et al., "Obesity and Obstructive Sleep Apnea: Pathogenic Mechanisms and Therapeutic Approaches," *Proceedings of the American Thoracic Society* 5, no. 2 (2008): 185–192, https://doi.org/10.1513/pats.200708-137MG.
22. Daniel E. Lieberman, *The Story of the Human Body: Evolution, Health, and Disease* (Vintage Books, 2014), 109.
23. "The Power of Prevention: Chronic Disease . . . the Public Health Challenge of the 21st Century," National Center for Chronic Disease Prevention and Health Promotion, 2009, https://stacks.cdc.gov/view/cdc/5509.
24. Eric Emerson et al., "Risk of Exposure to Air Pollution among British Children with and Without Intellectual Disabilities," *Journal of Intellectual Disability Research* 63, no. 2 (February 2019): 161–167, https://doi.org/10.1111/jir.12561.

25. Tesifón Parrón et al., "Association Between Environmental Exposure to Pesticides and Neurodegenerative Diseases," *Toxicology and Applied Pharmacology* 256, no. 3 (November 1, 2011): 379–385, https://doi.org/10.1016/j.taap.2011.05.006.
26. "Don't Pucker Up: Lead in Lipstick," Campaign for Safe Cosmetics, October 12, 2007, http://www.safecosmetics.org/about-us/media/news-coverage/dont-pucker-up-lead-in-lipstick/.

CHAPTER 5: WHEN BAD HABITS BECOME ADDICTIONS

1. Lee Ann Kaskutas, "Alcoholics Anonymous Effectiveness: Faith Meets Science," *Journal of Addictive Diseases* 28, no. 2 (2009): 145–157, https://doi.org/10.1080/10550880902772464.
2. "Artificially Sweetened Booze Packs More Punch," NBC News, May 23, 2006, https://www.nbcnews.com/id/wbna12939190.
3. Kate Janse Van Rensburg et al., "Acute Exercise Modulates Cigarette Cravings and Brain Activation in Response to Smoking-Related Images: An fMRI Study," *Psychopharmacology* 203, no. 3 (November 18, 2008): 589–598, https://doi.org/10.1007/s00213-008-1405-3.
4. Rachel L. Tomko et al., "N-Acetylcysteine: A Potential Treatment for Substance Use Disorders," *Current Psychiatry* 17, no. 6 (June 2018): 30–55, https://www.ncbi.nlm.nih.gov/pmc/articles/PMC5993450/.
5. Jon E Grant et al., "N-Acetyl Cysteine, a Glutamate-Modulating Agent, in the Treatment of Pathological Gambling: A Pilot Study," *Biological Psychiatry* 62, no. 6 (September 15, 2007): 652–657, https://doi.org/10.1016/j.biopsych.2006.11.021.

6. S. Jacob et al., "Oral Administration of Rac-α-Lipoic Acid Modulates Insulin Sensitivity in Patients with Type-2 Diabetes Mellitus: A Placebo-Controlled Pilot Trial," *Free Radical Biology & Medicine* 27, no. 3–4 (August 1999): 309–314, https://doi.org/10.1016/s0891-5849(99)00089-1.
7. See chapter 27, "Overeating Becomes More Dangerous," in David Kessler, *The End of Overeating: Taking Control of our Insatiable Appetite* (Penguin Books, 2010).
8. Byron Katie, *Loving What Is: Four Questions That Can Change Your Life* (Harmony Books, 2002).

APPENDIX 1: STRATEGIES FOR BETTER BRAIN HEALTH

1. Jun Sugawara et al., "Effect of Mirthful Laughter on Vascular Function," *American Journal of Cardiology* 106, no. 6 (September 15, 2010): 856–859, https://doi.org/10.1016/j.amjcard.2010.05.011.
2. Pedro Marques-Vidal and Virginia Milagre, "Are Oral Health Status and Care Associated with Anxiety and Depression? A Study of Portuguese Health Science Students," *Journal of Public Health Dentistry* 66, no. 1 (Winter 2006): 64–66, https://doi.org/10.1111/j.1752-7325.2006.tb02553.x.
3. Nancy L. Sin et al., "Daily Positive Events and Inflammation: Findings from the National Study of Daily Experiences," *Brain, Behavior, and Immunity* 43 (January 2015): 130–138, https://doi.org/10.1016/j.bbi.2014.07.015.
4. Meike Bartels, "Genetics of Wellbeing and Its Components Satisfaction with Life, Happiness, and Quality of Life: A Review and Meta-analysis of Heritability Studies," *Behavior Genetics* 45, no. 2

(March 2015): 137–156, https://doi.org/10.1007/s10519-015-9713-y.

5. Floriana S. Luppino et al., "Overweight, Obesity, and Depression: A Systematic Review and Meta-analysis of Longitudinal Studies," *Archives of General Psychiatry* 67, no. 3 (2010): 220–229, https://doi.org/10.1001/archgenpsychiatry.2010.2.
6. Centers for Disease Control and Prevention, "The Surprising Truth about Prediabetes," last reviewed May 15, 2024, https://www.cdc.gov/diabetes/prevention-type-2/truth-about-prediabetes.html.

ABOUT DANIEL G. AMEN, MD

Dr. Amen is a physician, board-certified child and adult psychiatrist, award-winning researcher, and 19-time national bestselling author. His online videos about brain and mental health have been viewed over half a billion times. Sharecare named him the web's No. 1 most influential expert and advocate on mental health, and the *Washington Post* called him the most popular psychiatrist in America.

He is the founder and CEO of Amen Clinics with locations nationwide. Dr. Amen is the lead researcher on the world's largest brain imaging and rehabilitation study on professional football players. His research has not only demonstrated high levels of brain damage in players, but also the possibility of significant recovery for many with the principles that underlie his work.

Together with Pastor Rick Warren and Dr. Mark Hyman, Dr. Amen is also one of the chief architects of The Daniel Plan, a program to get the world healthy through religious organizations that has been done in thousands of churches, mosques, and synagogues.

Dr. Amen is the author or coauthor of over 80 professional articles, 9 book chapters, and over 40 books, including 19 national bestsellers and 12 *New York Times* bestsellers, including the No. 1 *New York Times* bestseller *The Daniel Plan* and the over one million copy bestseller *Change Your Brain, Change Your Life*, which The VOU listed as one of the best self-help books of all time, along with *The End of Mental Illness*; *Healing ADD*; *Change Your Brain, Change Your Body*; *Memory Rescue*; *Your Brain Is Always Listening*; *You, Happier*; and *Change Your Brain Every Day*. His books have been translated into 46 languages.

Dr. Amen's published scientific articles have appeared in many prestigious scientific journals. In January 2016, his team's research on distinguishing PTSD from TBI on over 21,000 SPECT scans was featured as one of the top 100 stories in science by *Discover* magazine. In 2017, his team published a study on over 46,000 scans, showing the difference between male and female brains; and in 2018, his team published a study on how the brain ages on 62,454 SPECT scans.

Dr. Amen has written, produced, and hosted 18 national public television programs about brain health, which have aired more than 150,000 times across North America.

Dr. Amen has appeared in movies, including *Quiet Explosions*, *After the Last Round*, and *The Crash Reel* and was a consultant for *Concussion.* He appeared in the docuseries "Justin Bieber: Seasons" and has appeared regularly on *Dr. Phil* and *The Dr. Oz Show.* He has been featured on the *Today Show*, *Good Morning America*, *The Early Show*, CNN, Fox, and *The Doctors*, and appeared in the Emmy-winning show *The Truth About Drinking.*

In addition, Dr. Amen is one of the most visible and influential experts on brain health and mental health, with millions of followers on social media. Along with his wife, bestselling author

Tana Amen, he hosts the *Change Your Brain Every Day* podcast, which has ranked in the top 5 mental health podcasts and top 10 health podcasts overall. The podcast features thought leaders in the mental health field as well as high-profile actors, musical artists, athletes, entrepreneurs, and influencers.

He has also spoken around the world, with prestigious lectures in Canada, Brazil, Israel, and Hong Kong. He has spoken for the National Security Agency (NSA); the National Science Foundation (NSF); Harvard's Learning and the Brain Conference; the Department of the Interior; the National Council of Juvenile and Family Court Judges; the Supreme Courts of Ohio, Delaware, and Wyoming; and large corporations such as Merrill Lynch, Hitachi, Bayer Pharmaceuticals, GNC, NBA Referees, Miami Heat coaching staff; and many others. In 2016 Dr. Amen gave one of the prestigious Talks at Google.

Dr. Amen's work has been featured in the *New York Times*, the *New York Times Magazine*, *Washington Post Magazine*, *MIT Technology*, *Newsweek*, *Time*, *Huffington Post*, ABC World

News, *20/20*, BBC, *London Telegraph*, *Parade* magazine, *World Economic Forum*, *LA Times*, *Men's Health*, *Bottom Line*, *Vogue*, *Cosmopolitan*, *LA Style*, NPR, and many others.

In November 2017, an anonymous post of Dr. Amen's passion story (6 minutes) went viral and had over 40 million views. His two TEDx talks have more than 25 million views.

Dr. Amen is married to Tana, the father of six children, and grandfather to five. He is an avid table tennis player.